SUMMONING SHADES

Winner of the Adrienne Bond Poetry Award

Previous Winners

Seaborn Jones, *Going Farther into the Woods than the Woods Go*
(published 2012)

Kelly Whiddon, *The House Began to Pitch*
(published 2013)

Megan Sexton, *Swift Hour*
(published 2014)

Philip Lee Williams, *The Color of All Things: 99 Love Poems*
(published 2015)

Lesley Dauer, *Carnival Life*
(published 2016)

Katy Giebenhain, *Sharps Cabaret*
(published 2017)

Sara Pirkle Hughes, *The Disappearing Act*
(published 2018)

"Memory has one horizon," wrote George Seferis: R.T. Smith's superb new collection resonantly exemplifies this claim. Beginning with historical monologues and studies of characters as various as Mary Todd Lincoln, Audubon's assistant, and Patsy Cline, and ending with recollections from the author's own childhood, Smith refuses to draw a distinction between the historical past and the self as it negotiates the mysterious intricacies of memory. Like the tragic spiritualist Mary Todd Lincoln, Smith's aim is to summon up the dead, both the famous and the obscure, and to give them voice, allowing them to speak in a language that is at once vernacular and formally elegant. These are haunted, empathic, and durable poems, composed by a writer working at the height of his considerable powers.

—David Wojahn, author of *For the Scribe*

Hang on to your hors d'oeuvre, because this crush is a party. Everyone's here: Mary Lincoln flashing her new lace gloves, Lizzie toting her ax, and Audubon with his bloody birds. There's Meriwether Lewis sporting his bullet holes, and even Jerry Falwell whose heart gave out "after so much fried chicken / and inspiration." The entertainment? Patsy Cline in perfect pitch. The drink? Sparkling language straight from the punch bowl. And what a punch R. T. Smith has given us. It's one thing to know history, it's another to recreate it, call it up, and invite you to the party. I loved this book.

—Alice Friman, author of *The View from Saturn*

Among the many pleasures offered in *Summoning Shades,* as in each of R. T. Smith's collections, are the many years of his generous attention to nature, to the richness of Southern language and life, to music, and much more. One of his greatest gifts to us you can hear if you "listen with your/ heart's full force" / "voices elegant with lore and love."

—Don Selby, editor of *Poetry Daily*

SUMMONING SHADES

R. T. Smith

MERCER UNIVERSITY PRESS
Macon, Georgia
1979–2019
40 Years of Publishing Excellence

MUP/ P579

Published by Mercer University Press
1501 Mercer University Drive
Macon, Georgia 31207

9 8 7 6 5 4 3 2 1

Books published by Mercer University Press are printed on acid-free paper that meets the requirements of the American National Standard for Information Sciences—Permanence of Paper for Printed Library Materials.

Printed and bound in Canada.

This book is set in Adobe Caslon.

ISBN 978-0-88146-700-0
Cataloging-in-Publication Data is available from the Library of Congress

for Sarah

Contents

SUMMONING SHADES

1.

Mary Lincoln Suite

Gloves

October, 1862

Thrift, thrift Horatio . . . .

Spendthrift, you say? No, but also yes.
Entre nous: Finesse is everything, and if

I cover my fingers with precious fabric—calf
leather or velvet, silk of shantung
or charmeuse—my fine hands will dance,
despite all the jet and ebony of my mourning.

Sackcloth and ashes will not bring sweet Willie back,
and since I have drained bereavement's cup
and wept myself dry, the sprigs of funeral myrtle
are now forbidden. So I must uncocoon
and hide the martyr's face from my surviving boys.
Let Victoria remain the priestess of misery;
I will display a survivor's poise,
keep Tad and Robert by my side
as I visit afflicted soldiers from the killing fields.

But every spending spree, mind you, is designed
to distract from migraines like thunderstorms
within me. Less mania than calculation,
my millinery outings with retinue and etiquette
preserve me, and I have my advocates:
poor sons too good to dwell on this unworthy earth,
Eddie and Willie both in séance somberly

entreat: mother do not neglect
elegance, which amplifies both your elevated station

and grief itself. Lizzie Keckley (who knows
the White House staff call me "Hellcat"
for my tantrums, which are not excessive)
says this: custom gloves are the luxuries the senators'
ladies will likely eye with most envy,

ribboned gloves, those open at the wrist with pearl buttons,
dove-colored, Chantilly, seamed, hush-blue, those suited
for the opera or riding, mittens for frost, every cut and cloth,
gloves … and fans—the Italian, the Japanese laced
with figures like fantastic shadows and spreading
wing-like with one flick of my wrist. Because Father
shares his many secrets and seeks advice,

calls me his "Kitchen Cabinet," they hate me,
all the pullets in their leg-o-mutton sleeves
and empire waists. I am woven like a silken thread
in jacquard through this war,

and they but bystanders, jackals under their bonnet
brims, such halos of the ordinary I have to laugh.

> Sometimes in the Green Room I see Willie and nearly
> lose all resolve—but pinch my wrist, stiffen up.

How they would outdo me, though,
with damask floral patterns, ashes-of-rose
and parlor wit, but I am more eloquent in French,
which few can match. I will teach
them how we scorn in Illinois, and I can glare
across a soirée with lethal frost,

or exchange candid glances with the sovereign
of this whole nation, flutter my gloved fingers in a wave,
that Mr. Lincoln may smile amid his woes.

Grief: no more frill and fringe.
Leave the canary yellow, magenta flounce
and cobweb shawl to the hussies of the punch bowl,
harridans of the whisper and politesse.

Yet I sustain my smile. Noblesse oblige? *Oubliette.*

Debt, of course, hovers,
and in private, without his corvid uniform
and cannon hat, he will admonish me: Pray, Mother,
how can I pay Haughwout's, Galt's Emporium, Mr. Stewart,
and all the rest of your glovers while our soldiers
in the field have no blankets?

But his heart knows we are a symbol and must shine.

Silhouette and embellishment now, without the rainbow,
yet they will flatter me, say I ravish the eye
with my bell shape and grace, my reticent attire. A lie,
yet my purple iris overlay, passing
for sable, puts their rose and emerald in the shade.

Last night I overheard
Mr. Lincoln confide to Seward, "Her flub-a-dubs
overwhelm me. Her shopping will stink in the land,"
but what are eighteen pairs of gloves
when he commands millions
to be spent, and not for love. Shoes and boots again,
madam, he complains, but no bloodshed follows me,
no *fleuve sanglant*, and neither amethyst broach

nor tiered sleeve ever set the pandemonium torch

to any city. That harpy Mercy Conkling has dubbed me
"Her Royal Highness," and the screech owl Hannah
Blaine hisses "Madame Excess," though I do love pearls
and fresh jasmine, dining on duck and terrapin—
Parisian, but all in just proportion.

How few understand the heavy hours, how deeply
I went into weeping for my boys,
but I am recovered enough to know a First Lady
must astonish the vox populi and bask.

In taffeta silks and velvet, all my fine blacks,
I'll act the basilisk.
First the slow smolder,
but a sheathed hand can flash faster than the eye
and consign the gossips to ice
or the flames of Satan.

Once again the migraine sparks beneath my
picturesque *coronet noire*, my private burden.
Willie's face swirls in a marble pattern. What solution?

Thrift? Thank you, no, not this grande dame.
I'll promenade, spit fire. Somehow I'll thrive.

Summoning Shades

St. Catherine's Spa, Canada: June, 1873

Willie had come forth as all in our spirit circle
of clasped hands watched a candle flicker like forsythia
in wind, yet the air was still. His voice was an echo,
a soft song wafting through water.
He told us of endless bluebell meadows
and ripe cherries falling into his hands.
He said Tad was with him now among the shades, and I was
forgiven all my parties and other adult follies.

Veiled, I sail under false flags to test every mystic,
that they will not guess my famous sons and Mr. Lincoln
are the voices I eagerly seek. Can I trust them at all,
my faculties so shaken by grief?

Last night Frau Lili Hausman seemed honest enough,
a genuine vehicle, until the sudden disruption.

Willie floated on the verge of a revelation
when we startled at a knock, not from beyond
but at the door, and in moments lantern beams flooded
the sacred chamber: our medium was seized
and arrested by royal constables for fraud and theft
of a necklace. Heaven help us.

The bereft are vulnerable as leverets in the nest.

Of course, we all admit the speculative arts are rife
with charlatans. As any wit can see: we who seek messages
from Summerfield are desperate, which does not mean

we are misguided. Listen:

I have trembled in darkened parlors, watching the ectoplasm
rise to duplicate faces of the departed—
one doctor's jonquil of a daughter,
a weeping Quaker's husband fallen under a trolley in Boston.
Lord knows Mr. Lincoln took his skepticism

to the grave, but now he hovers above me, an angel
christened by misfortune. He often fills the vessel
of the medium and says, "Take heart."

I sometimes wish less fortunate war widows
could pilgrim this far north to see Niagara's great weeping
and find comfort in the cataracts, which shimmer
with white mist that could be a portal to our darlings,
despite the scoffing of cynics who say a séance is theater
for simpletons. Friends and enemies alike claim
clairvoyance is no more honest than a carnival mirror.
Even dearest Robert, who mutes
his disapproval . . . but I can guess those storms behind his eyes.
Who knows his true heart?

Scripture records the intimates of Job counted his suffering just,
reasoning, as he bathed in dust, he must have sinned deeply,
but how have I deserved such wealth of loss?

If the dead have answers, why not ask?

And if our rites are merely drama, with their hush
and curtains, shadow play and suspension
of disbelief . . . why, we make Tragedy
reverse—Lear howling for his precious dove,
Hecuba mourning her many sons as she transforms to a hound—

had they faith, they would know eternal peace
and pursue its mysteries. It is not sickness. At least
Sally Orde and Myra Bradwell stand by me and see
in this seeking some dignity,
which is not easy when the body heaves with sobs,
and even in the face of public ridicule
the essence yearns for release.

  But last night was a low moment,
as speechless, we watched the constables twist the key
in Lili's manacles, and I wondered that the spirit guides
could not assist her, as her features
assumed a tragic mask. Before the officers left,
the necklace was seized, a wondrous circle of gems

so deep their green was nearly night. Explanations
may be forthcoming, but is there not distress
enough in our corporeal realm to satisfy any demon?
No doubt my name will soon see newsprint again.

Everyone asserts the history of this endeavor is twisted,
and now the Fox sisters who first heard spirit telegraphy
have confessed to deceit, but others are authentic
and desire not to swindle so much as unleash the healing secrets.
  Mr. Mumler, for instance, whom I visited just this year
under the *nom de guerre* of Mrs. Tydall,
never guessed my identity, and detected nothing unusual
through the lens, but when he lifted the silver print
from its chemical fixer, he was amazed as I
to see Mr. Lincoln clearly visible behind me, hands resting
on my shoulders in his former fashion, face placid
in death. The image was unmistakable, and I have copies yet
to overwhelm the skeptics who shall set in
like wolves to discredit Mumler's conjury as "counterfeit."

Possession and loss—we all learn the sequence,
but how we suffer who could not honor the gods of proportion.

The Lauries of Georgetown told me: "Mary, your excess
is selfish, it is time to resume living," even as they summoned Father
from the crepuscular beyond, and Nettie Colburn's
usual guide Pinkie assured me the President
was happier where no cabinet traitors
plotted against him and called him "our gorilla" in secret.
He awaits only my arrival to complete his serenity,
as they dwell in an Elysian demesne, and their only worry
is the safety of those stranded this side of the river.

Is it not great comfort for a starved heart to feel the departed
surround you as a cloud? That is my sensation
in mid-trance. I, also, doubt
much of the rattling and automatic writing, the jingling bells,
aromas to stimulate memory, but voices of my boys
and husband are another matter. I am soothed but can never
hear enough and afterwards yearn to journey beyond the veil.

Even visitations in Europe yielded little succor,
as Mr. Lincoln appeared above a Tuscan chapel's altar,
and I followed Tad, then little Eddie through winding
Kinderstrauss in Baden-Baden, their laughter
as from the past playing tag through our own labyrinth
now occupied by that butcher Grant,
who has seemed unmoved by so much slaughter.
I always drink in the sounds of my beloved
like a desert absorbing water.
Tonight I will again in secret approach death's threshold—
the cool mists and hushes around a skirted table
where we form a human wreath

hoping the shadows will consent to speak.

If twilight must become my one safe haven on earth,
it is fitting. After all, I was born a Todd,
and *tod* in German says "death,"
which Willie promises nightly is sweeter than any sleep.

A Serpent's Tooth

May, 1876   Springfield, Illinois

I held my tongue, though even in shock,
that is not my nature,
but this morning a bluebird is singing Union blue
in the orchard, his feathers the core of a gas jet's
flame. At last I can journey back
to my indictment and captivity, the suffering my one
surviving son inflicted. A year. I will not say his name.
Hell is in my heart, but madness was never my burden.

Could croquet and hammocks, carriage rides
and endless tea, rose gardens to rival the Tuilleries tame
the truly demented? Atmosphere was everything, civility,
but Dr. Patterson's remedies were just the sort of sham
men forever devise to fetter an able woman's capacities,
and they will always style it chivalry.

I confess to torturous headaches, joints aflame, palpitations,
the fitting grief of one who has lost so many.
And was Mrs. Lincoln "prone to purchase in excess,
then grow desperate concerning money?"
Yes, I tried to sell the costumes meant to make a First Lady
inspiring. I sewed bonds into my petticoats
but also endured fevers and weeping—
my muscles burning, the shakes, my running waters.
They gave me Squibb chloral hydrate in bitter solution,
which kept me close to lethargy,
and I shrieked back only in spirit when admonished.
History's widows have been prone to ailments few others
can fathom. Woe to those who must "seek asylum."

The condition, in French, is *aliénation*. Precisely.

But set it all aside, even if I did see spies at every corner
(and now know the Pinkertons and servants lurked,
RTL's agents seeking to record every gesture).
Did that make me Pandora?

Tomorrow marks the anniversary,
and he is once again devising petitions to return me
to that Bellevue Plantation for the Off-Kilter and Crazed
(not, of course, the name they dare display on the gate,
nor the bucolic brochures of ivied lies).

And so they came, Mr. Leonard Swett and his officers,
to lead me straight—in handcuffs—into court to answer
charges. In the Windy City the law requires any persons suspected
of unsound mind be indicted with the crime
of insanity—note: the *crime*. So long as the bluebird
spirits from tree to tree I can disclose the horrors.
No one spoke for me, my own counsel sharing
the conviction that I was *non compos mentis*,
required supervision to prevent me from self-harm,
and I was supposed a danger even to loved ones. Barristers
and solicitors, evidence given by clerks and notaries,
sums and inventories—all that masculine quackery was mustered
to put me away. The Bard has an answer for lawyers.
And the doctors in their whiskers were in the main
men I had never met, though they rattled off such diagnoses!

For finale, my son spoke through sobs, the cost
to him of holding the sacred legacy and estate
of his beloved father intact. I was bringing disgrace
and scandal to the national memory.
"Pound foolish," he said, in his pious voice, "of unsound reason,"

"a peril to herself and others." Judas boy.
And all for the sake of silver, this *Grand Guignol.*

Hopeless, I did not ascend the stand, half afraid
they would hold my Kentucky tongue against me,
as RTL sat there, his elf ears and high collar, a local civic pillar
with his official accent bland as clabber.
And it would not have mattered an inch or an ounce,
as already the newspapers were tomahawking me sans mercy:
"The Demented Widow," "A Nation's Shame."

Ten minutes of deliberation
served to draw their consensus conclusion:
guilty, and sentenced to exile of undisclosed duration.
Can those silk tongues not know how seeming lunacy
may mask a divine lucidity? But why even ask?

Outside pastoral Batavia Dr. Patterson reigned
over Bellevue Place, the tenants including:
Mrs. Wheeler who ranted at dawn and pounded the floor by night,
Mrs. Edouard who would not desert her bed,
Mrs. Mungar who stabbed herself with the matron's scissors,
Mrs. Johnson who urinated on the floors in the name of God,
Mrs. Harcourt who raved and died on the premises,
poor Minnie Judd who had to be force-fed,
so desperate was she to disappear,
and then the notorious Mrs. Lincoln, whose ungrateful son
learned at Harvard to justify his every writ and edict.
Words may "fly up to heaven," yet come from another realm.

My bed, stylish, expensively ornate,
my room private, but for the hireling spinster
Elvira Ross, ingratiating but mouse-devious,
who watched me through slats at all hours.

I rocked in my comfortable chair or wrote letters,
toured the manicured grounds and conspired with my visitors
cunning as Mrs., Surratt, who kept the nest
that sheltered Booth and all his vipers.
Does such sinister comparison convey my desperation?

It was in the garden that the bluebirds first addressed me
amid the early irises frilled like petticoats,
and what they promised was freedom,
on the condition I renounce revenge. My instructions:
simply conduct yourself as if this charade were normal,
converse with muted animation,
hands clenched in your lap or busy knitting,
and follow the regimen with smiles. In short: captivate
your captors and never speak of anguish
over who has your trunks and how that nameless martinet
conducts the business of your funds,
all in the name of devotion and pity.

Restrained behavior saved me from the chemical cures
favored in that chateau of torture:
opium, morphia, cannabis, indica, belladonna,
ergot, conium and Bellevue's celebrated whisky-laced eggnog,
all dispensed to suspend the patients in harmonious lassitude.
J'ai parlé avec les mortes,
and they will tell you mental energy is the essential elixir
for both sides of the cosmic river,
so I feign stupor but keep my quiet lightning.

Robert. There, I have said it. Robber, covert,
my monster of mankind son. His confederates
knew that voices swirled inside my head and I feared fire
beyond proportion. They amplified my symptoms
till even dear sister Elizabeth agreed it best to cozy me

in a "secure place," safe for devotees of Duty.
Even in my loony room I had to endure a sentry,
Miss Ross of the soft voice who watched me like a hawk,
and from my bluebird's whispers, I know, no mouse at all.

Now I have this terrace, no leash, the so-called freedom
of a woman wronged, then settled with caring kin.
Even the army of my enemies agree,
despite the serpent's bite, I no longer flash the aspect
of a dangerous woman, though I know
the lay of the land, country of sanity I never left.

And still the bluebird sings to me *doucement*,
brings dispatches from beyond, and the connivers
of "justice" have never guessed I have a pistol,
my one white trunk stored at the station and ready
for escape—a hooded cloak, emeralds, gowns, the Todd silver.
Ah, *mon petit ouiseau bleu* flashing in the sky,
will they surprise me again? "Restored to reason"—
that lets them all sleep easily. And remorse? Not guilty.

Midday now, birdsong, and in the distance smoke twirls
the hue of a fawn in winter, color its only
defense. Folded in my green rouche sleeve I keep my final
retribution—the will, witnessed and signed lovingly,
"Your dearest Mother." Let him finally comprehend and suffer
the sting: I will leave him all.

Lizzie Keckley, '91

A woman written out of history, though handsome
and the colors of an acorn, caressing her sewing
basket by the window, as if musing on the late sun's russet,
a peach pit, a snarl of yarn.

The ladies Davis and Lee and Lincoln—I have been
seamstress to queens. Her hands rise to autumn light,
still strong, but never steady unless wielding a needle.

Thin as a spindle, she won't make it a full century
but is not sundowning yet and thinks clear as a spring:
It was the saddest quarrel. I only tried to shine
a brighter light on her nature.
I wanted to bring her sympathy and relief.

Authoress of *Behind the Scenes* to show the private pain
of a wartime White House, to rescue her unlikely
friend from newsboys in the street crowing the headlines:
SCANDAL. A NATIONAL SPECTACLE. FORMER FIRST
LADY
ATTEMPTS TO SELL DRESSES. SHAME.
Through agents
of Brady & Keyes, Mary Todd offered Chantilly shawls, gowns,
sabled gloves, and parasol covers. Desperate
not to be destitute, and her longtime companion—
born a slave but able by sheer grit, art, and labor
to earn her freedom—raised a voice in pity, but the wits
and partisans saw spite in the pages, betrayal,
and Mrs. Lincoln soon agreed.
I never meant the letters to go in.
So sorrowful, so wrong, and I never saw her again.

The needle slips into white cotton, pulling dark thread through.

She takes coffee with chicory and tries not to dwell
on that national disgrace and the rift
she felt so deeply, just as she endeavors to forget the whip
and seeing her kind sold, like hogs, by the pound.

Quick as a finch, precise, her fingers could mend a hem, run
a seam, rouche a sleeve while she listened.
She never neglected to listen.
She'd served in field and kitchen—the hoe, the picking sack,
skillets big as the moon, burns from sun and grease and steam—
learned the milliner's art in secret—loop stitch and common
stitch, taut now, knot and bite clean—at her mother's knee.

I was privy to her headaches, the manias, and scorn
she endured for being so-called "southern."
"Modiste" is what they call a servant who dresses the lady.
I would come at any hour she summoned me—rain, sleet,
the street rowdy with soldiers. Anything,
any mission, even to match a fabric swatch. Modiste
and more, I watched her stumble from grief to grief.

She said the needle put bread in her mouth,
kith and kin as all the white ladies
sought her favors: Mrs. Bonnet, Madame Flounce, Her Worship
the High Bustle—all polite as preachers
when they wanted elegance, a proper pleat.

    She might be sawtoothing gingham
with her pinking shears or on her knees, squinting,
lips clenching pins as she adjusted the ruffs and trim
of cobweb lace while Mary Lincoln herself
said, "Keckley, I need your advice."

The First Lady would bare excesses and regrets, pillow talk
from her husband, while Lizzie wondered, "Can a whole life,
a whole nation be slipped through the bright eye
of a needle?"

She'd lost a husband, also a son passing as white
in Union blue but kept her own secrets
wound tight about a spool and spoke with the hush
of brushed linen: "Mrs. Lincoln, I know that man Father
Abraham is God's angel. We're all in his hands.
You've got to trust him, even when he's peculiar,
even when no earthly other can understand."

Snip, measure and measure, snip again. Even now her fingers,
nervous as birds when idle,
can run a licked thread through the shiny eye.

Lordy, but we suffered together, whispered
like wind under a sill. Now she pauses and lifts
a thimble's gleam to the dying light. Listen now:
It's still that old wind a-whistle,
and then her fingers are frightened sparrows again.

You take what the world gives you
in His wisdom and sew it to what you need.
Smiling, as her head nods forward.
The vigor of steel is evident
in her features as she sutures the fabric of sleep.

Mockingbird

(Gettysburg: November, 1863)

That next autumn the Weaver Brothers
with their camera bigger than a hatbox
caught us at Bull's tavern in parade dress
half-snockered on cheap oh-be-joyful.
They promised each man a half dollar
to pose on Devil's Den where the slaughter
we'd survived in the recent summer
had been too gruesome to summon
to mind full sober. So we trooped out
into the brisk weather and reclined,
artful as a squad of studio models
tricked out as the dead, while a pair
of doctors in smart frock coats stood
over us like Satan's angels claiming
souls on the threshold. "It's all theater,"
jested the photographer's helper,
now that Lincoln and the multitudes
had remembered and cheered and gone,
but I'd been there for the big scrap—
crouching, shit-scared, firing wild.
I couldn't quit flinching, not back in July
nor in the cold and quiet. Our Corporal
Billikin, knock-kneed in his cups, kept
singing from his ghost pose a popular
ditty called "Listen to the Mockingbird,"
about the bird trilling high in the willow
by the grave of poor Halle. "We want
the look of fresh dead," one Weaver
shouted out from under his camera hood:

"Cut out the hayseed concert, fellow,
and pretend asleep, if feigning death
seems to you reckless." It was reckless,
but I was soused and sprawled across
the altar of the pinnacle rock to watch
empty limbs pointing out our tableau's
lie: not summer at all, but frosty season.
Fool Billikin kept warbling his somber
song, as if it was a funeral, as if we'd
not all soon head back to the tavern's fire.
Making history again, we were glad
to be among the living still, damn glad,
but Sergeant Archer scolded the boy
to drop his chirping: "Secesh marched
out to that tune. It's a killer's rhythm."
And suddenly we were all cold sober,
avoiding each other's eyes, dead solemn.
We'd had all the art a man could bear.

Still Life: from the Notebooks of A. Bierce, 1862

After Antietam, with smoke still scumbling the air,
the *Harpers* artist paced away
from the Sunken Road where a full brigade
had been strafed and decimated.
The flies had begun to swarm, lighting on the eyes
and open wounds of the fallen, the stench
already gut-wrenching, heart-rending,
as were the groans of injured pack animals
weighted down by tack and baggage,
as well as that last shadow beasts can divine,

but the artist spread out his charcoals and chalk
on a blue blanket and leaned against the trunk
of a smoking blackjack pine.
The Rebel rear guard occasionally launched a volley,
as Federal cooks gathered wood to ready the mess
in case any survivors could muster a hunger.

Stroke by stroke, the draftsman began his sketch,
three peaches slowly forming, their delicacy almost sexual,
shade and shadow, amplitudes unblemished, colors
of dawn fire and sunset, the fuzz nearly palpable
enough to make the skin itch,
scent so nearly visceral my tongue
and lips went moist whispering "peach."
An Illinois corporal peering over the artist's shoulder
broke his silence to say, "Fellow, can't you see
all them soldiers blown apart or in misery right here?
How the hell can you ignore the horses,
the jack mules, that wagon yonder still in flames?
Peaches? What the hell?"
But the correspondent kept his focus, summoning

the delicious, the elegant repose
in earshot of the surgeon's tent, the work of the saw
and the miserable screaming, where the faces of casualties
were twisted and hideous. Orderlies
splattered in blood rushed about weeping. An officer
with an eye badly patched oversaw the burial
detail spading dirt into the trench already filling
with scrapped bandages and grisly limbs.
"'Still life,' we art makers say," was the sketch artist's answer,
"meaning both 'motionless' and 'not yet dead,'
though the phase after ripeness is not so lovely,
and the pit clenched in the fruit's core
is redder than carnage, rougher
than your musket balls, a full bore
.54 caliber, if I reckon correctly,"

And then he looked from the soldier's angry eyes
to the empty sky before he resumed.

"Peaches, maybe, are what I need to see, what my weary
heart yearns to remember.
Better than any green shoots or delicate petals,
better than family toasts and a sister deft at the piano,
I know the bloodbath we inhabit, sir,
against which I can offer only a fragile
moment as counterpoint to our surround.
Here's the reason, I would imagine, the French call
such compositions, whether fruit or meat
or a vase of mint sprigs and zinnias, *nature mort*.
The merest feast of grace, all
there is, as there is no remnant God,
no other rebuttal to trust,
while even Pity wears a mantel of feeding flies."

Just a witness, I held my tongue but had no more appetite
for the taste of his beautifully rendered fruit.

And the corporal's retort?
"Mister, get yourself a rifle,
see if you can still puke out them jackass lies."

Henry Kyd Douglas, After Cold Harbor

It is not war that makes us mortal
nor courage that sows this subtraction,
but something infernal in the Design
that rises when the skirmish line—
just after a volley—wavers and thins,
then rights the colors and closes ranks,
while shells whistle over, demented,
and trees burst into furied flame.
The stench of seared horse flesh
and spent powder haunts the air.

This morning, sweeping my long glass
across a hillside, surveying to assess
last night's damage, I realized I could tell
our pitiful dead from the Federals
at a fair distance in high summer,
as they are well fed and full of juices,
while our starved volunteers are all
sinew and sparse gristle, still intact
as they festoon the bitter field.
The northern lads swell and suppurate,
though it did not escape my notice—
listening to the rear guard's rifles
and hearing distant artillery's random
retort—that the azure butterflies
lured from the forest show no bias
and alight on the upturned faces
of either army's fallen boys
to sip the ichor from their eyes.

Flower Coffin, 1864

Not mahogany, but pine and painted white,
edges beveled and the handles pure silver,
the traditional tapered shape, and candles

as yet unlit on a frame outside the border,
so of course the child on the bed of petals
is porcelain white and stiff as the doll

at her shoulder. Dressed as a bride, angel
or spun sugar treat, she does not smile,
and the lining of silk is pale as gossamer,

the only color a scarlet hint on her lips,
which may remind the file of mourners
how the speck of red touched her temple

when most of the cannon had ceased to roar
and a rain sonata was tapping the summer
leaves, as if to signal the end of all battle.

Even the pony-drawn hearse by the door
is white, but the stiff jacket and trousers
worn by her brother are dark as gunpowder,

and the bone button at his neck no larger
than the wandering shard of burning metal
that surprised this sister who was running,

laughing, barking back at her silver spaniel
through blue flowers softer than feathers
on what was called the safe side of the river
where quietly she fell. Her name was Pearl.

Major Henry Rathbone

I spoke with him once the autumn after
the assassin gashed him, shouted his slogan
and fled down the April alleys of the capital.
He had been—by our chilly afternoon
reunion—mustered out, of course, and lacking
the uniform in which he'd looked so dashing,
he seemed again a boy, but with posture slack
and movements sluggish. Yet in his eyes a fire
gleamed. I would deign to call it excitement
but wondered why he smoldered still,
as in school he had kept the coolest head,
even when our masters wielded the cane.
We envied his panache but could never
quite admire that mysterious reserve.

He shouldered much of the blame, despite
his presence in the presidential box
being wholly accidental: a battlefield major
relegated at last to desk work, he was a guest,
unarmed, savoring the gala atmosphere,
and doting on Miss Harris. Their plans
to wed were just recently public, the blush
still on the rose. The president had blessed them,
and no one mentioned they were step-siblings
and had chosen a path not widely approved.
I see him now as in a tintype—loose cravat,
sideburns, traveling jacket and pearl shirt,
his hat brim ever-circling in tense fingers.

"They said she flung goldfish in her tantrums,"
he said of Miss Keane, the diva that spring night.

“They called her ‘the Duchess’ in secret. On stage,
she seemed quite calm.” But he did not and began
to twist his new derby so roughly I asked
to hold it and praised the maker—John Cavendish,
Boston, Gentleman’s Apparel. “It was a farce
with mangled language and imbecile British;
I have seldom relished the theater’s mischief,”
he volunteered, then suddenly stared hard
into the pressed tin ceiling and whispered,
“Would you care to view my wound.” Booth’s knife—
he said it was bright as a regimental whistle—
had rent him from elbow to shoulder, and before
I could demur, he was unhooking his cuff,
saying, “Delicate buttons of bone.” The scar
was white as a maggot, and then: “I believe
the rogue uttered ‘freedom’ as he slashed me.
Is it not strange? ‘Freedom?’” And that was it,
our brief audience abruptly at an end.
He covered the arm and snatched his damaged
hat from me like one retrieving a talisman
but rose weakly, as if shaken by the sight
of his injury. “It was gun smoke, you know,
all in my eyes, the shrieking like ripped copper.
The starlet was dressed in canary attire.
The president was laughing like a jackal.
I had no chance to prevent the worst murder
God has allowed.” I tried to offer solace,
to remind him of Booth’s end and promise
a beautiful future with the Senator’s
daughter. He was already elsewhere, though,
eyes crossing. “Blood wedding,” he replied.
“It will carry the stain.”

I am told there was
an ermine edge on Mrs. Lincoln's satin
jacket and that Rathbone somehow tore it
free that night and would not surrender the item
when she later sent inquiries, but that
is only rumor, and I wish to cling to facts
as I know them. He was nearly thirty
but seemed, that day, sixteen and tipsy. Perhaps
so much bleeding had worked a change. You see,
it was his blood that made Miss Harris swoon
and so shocked Laura Keen. An artery nicked
and spraying as he grappled the assassin.
The divans and curtains were stained in it,
the president himself and his evening shawl,
the First Lady's frock, the executive flag.
Some say even the shadows.

I finished my sherry
slowly and chose not to follow him
into the rainy street, for I was unnerved
and feared what might become of a man
so stricken. In truth, there had been no worry
at all for Lincoln's safety on such occasions.
Soldiers were usually about as couriers
and embellishment only, and he resisted
escorts of Pinkertons he thought gun thugs
for hire. No fault but in our general hubris,
for which we all must shoulder our fair share
and no more, not even our poor Henry.

Though deeply ill, he married Clara and fathered
three children, but could not settle. The family
traveled on the continent from one grand spa
to another, seeking some storybook idyll.

He was finally, briefly, Grover Cleveland's
consul to Hanover—nervous at court,
inept with the language and protocols,
but decked in medals. By eighty-one, Madam
Rathbone told intimates his fits of temper
featured threats, that he was idle and she
disdained divorce only for the children's sake,
yet I was still among those who never
guessed the ending.

One Christmas Eve morning
she woke at dawn to find him dressed, pacing
like a sentry. When he asked to see his sons,
she refused, citing the early hour, and tried
to soothe him with tea. He shot her stone dead,
then stabbed himself—such irony!—when a nurse
prevented him from harming his offspring. His end?
A room in the old St. Michael Asylum
in Hiedelshiem, cursing vapors he believed
seeping from stone walls to addle his brain
and drawing endless pencil sketches of Yule
trees decked in ornaments, or so I assume,
for last I heard he's living still, no doubt
dreaming the stage heroine's yellow dress
or Booth's impressive riding suit, and raving
about sinister gasses and the mortal sin
of marrying his sister, each syllable spoken
sotto voce, and all in schoolboy German,
the only language I bested him at far back
when we galloped about the town, raising
Cain, waving our birch sabers in savage arcs
and saying we were warrior brothers
who would save our sacred nation from the dark.

Impasto

In Winslow Homer's "A Visit from the Old Mistress,"
the three black women gaze at the plantation's
"lady"—now graying but still carefully coiffed,
straight as a pine and necklaced in rescued lace.

The hostesses in their homespun almost blend
with worn wood and smoked stone of the kitchen.
Their dresses dyed the shades of earth and birds
are dingy, piecemeal but stitched with dignity—

Anna-Dovey? perhaps Clarice? In her quarter
of the canvas Madam wears a dress for mourning.
"Mistus" they call her to her face, but no chair
has been offered nor chicory to ease her thirst.

From the shadows, yet no longer in them, the trio
hold their ground in sharp profile. The guest's
expression may indicate self-pity, or the art
of doing without—brandy wine, violas, Spode,

her beloved show pony now dragging a plow.
Every keepsake thrown down the well or privy
was found, hauled off to adorn a foreign parlor,
and she thinks of this state as "starting over,"

as asking where once a sharp gaze sufficed.
She still cannot read their silence.
                                        The fifth face
is a babe's, thank God too young to have been
her late husband's get. Like its elders the infant

beholds her without flinching. All women,
but too much misery between them for “sister”
to pass their lips. Homer has allowed no space
for step or gesture, the whole tableau wrought

in French oils brushed rough, tinged with dirge
and bistre, then gouged in paste pigments.
If only some chimney swift would flutter in
and startle them awake, then the earth might turn

and breath be released. Yet here they stand,
unable to resist this impasse. The merciful angel
they need may never come. The artist might
as well have carved them in ice or granite.

History lies heavy as a bullet on the tongue.

2.

Mendicant No More: Joseph Mason, 1848

for Brendan Galvin

1.
No genius myself, I was not without talent,
and soon Audubon heaped praises, saying
I could charm a vine to flower on the page.
Honeysuckle, I believe, was the sketch in question,
and by dint of that effort he said, "Join me, then,
as I seek specimens in the wild sky to preserve
their patterns and habitat. We shall duplicate
the Lord's wondrous craft." So I apprenticed
and learned to mirror his beliefs on "nature,"
his favorite word. I spoke it back and learned
to crouch frog-wise in marshes so quiet and still
the very self appeared to vanish, and I was
often his porter when we left the skiff to enter
the tangled, warbling world. I daily labored
to keep our fowling pieces loaded with mustard
shot, so as not to deface the birds he would
prop and dispose to counterfeit life. With Ohio
long behind, I worked the *Columbia's* galley,
and scrubbed pots, my flute echoing the master's
trills. Under the live oaks looming ghostly
with Spanish beard, I knew my business. Near
Yazoo I gave chase, then shot a cormorant, head
and neck rising from the murk like a snake.
Hornbeam I drew for his backdrops, may apple
and *semper vivens* jessamine, calyx and tendril.

I'll not deny he was my mentor, and I quickly
came to love him as a father, nor did I question
then the abundance with which he knocked
his sacred birds from the sky, but after Oakley
the bond between us soured, for he would not
so much as pen into his ledger which pictures
I supplied with plant and ambiance. "Mr. Jsf.
Mason" he scrawled on rare occasion in crayon,
fading as soon as set, while he inked in India
his own name, staking eternal claim. The ribbon
sedge, for instance, his prairie warblers bend
with their perching: anonymous to the future,
yet necessary to fabricate fierce atmosphere.
Every twist and bristle, that work was mine.

2.
In New Orleans we struggled, nibbling cheese
and cheap mackerel, while he peddled his finesse
at quick portraiture with black chalk. I ground
colors, rinsed brushes in spirits and scavenged
while he courted the prosperous, eager to please
their wives as I to retain his favor. Some days
we forayed amid the alligator swamps and saw
ivory bills in the cypress, the gallinule, umber
diver, buntings and snipe, boat-tailed grackles,
and among them warblers he called "battleground,"
though later I learned it was another of his vain
inventions: no such species exists. Two incidents
of note occurred before we left the Crescent.
He rendered a lady now called "The Fair
Incognito," likely another mistress of Marigny,
and said, almost swooning, he drew her nude,
then swore to Lucy nothing passed between them
but conversation, a single civil kiss. The tariff

she offered was the price of a Greener shotgun
inlaid and bearing inscriptions. Although I guess
little and can prove less, my master was a man
of appetites—handsome, animated, dashing—his
russet locks flowing *á la chevalier*, eyes always
flashing, and I doubt not some dalliance of strong
affect ensued. He was cunning and selfish. Not
for nothing he often signed himself "LaForest,"
and his stories might sacrifice even their tithe
of truth for effect. Famous as a liar, he cared not
who knew. "What I fathom of nature," he said,
"would engulf them." Our departure from the city
of miasma and intrigue was no doubt hastened
by a certain Mrs. Heermann's "rude accusation"
that while delivering her sketching lessons
the Birdslayer made advances. He denied all,
claiming the reverse, like Joseph in the tale
of Potiphar's wife. I did not like to hear
my Christian name so invoked, but he was still
my comrade and had promised me ample portion
of the impending fame. New Orleans became
a Bedlam, and I believed him a victim of ploys
and misfortune. Evenings his hands trembled.
Ailing, he needed the berry Renzo Newcomb
said can remedy malaise. Epistles from home
had turned stormy. The loss of two daughters
brought night sweats, haunting his every thought.
Moreover, our daily fare had sunk so low we shared
a gumbo of barred owl with neighbors (bearable
with ample hunger and much pepper). He catered
to the vain, but the fees were still too meager.
"We must escape or die," he declared. Then our
luck turned, and he soon dazzled Madame Pirrie
of Feliciana. So we embarked on the derelict

Ramapo, our pockets nearly empty. In Bayou
Sarah a room awaited us in the cellar of elegant
Oakley. There Monsieur would teach the girl
Miss Eliza to dance, elocute and paint, while
I would fetch and study or mix pigments,
but there a business of shadows altered all,
and it is not to my credit that I held my tongue.

3.
A paradise at first, the air shivered with song.
Woodcock, thrush, grosbeak, and cuckoo, rail
and larks, while splendid Delta kites circled
above. In bliss we listened and shot, sketched
and dissected. The girl was hardly a natural
but sought the divine in every claw and feather.
Madame Pirrie, something of an apothecary, laid
a fine table, and her spouse was blithe company
when not mastered by Haitian rum. After dinner,
it's being summer, we enjoyed pipes on the portico
and tossed French hazard with dice. Other guests
begged him for entertainment, so the Raconteur
treated us to stories I knew better than to believe,
but in truth we preferred solitude with field notes,
penning epistles by candle. When word arrived
of my father's demise, Audubon provided heart's
ease and kept me occupied. By day Lizzie's
refinement was our mission, and I confess I never
noted anything to pass between tutor and student
other than decorum allows. If betimes he called
her "darling," such was his practice with many.
And yet, approaching autumn, tensions arose
between artist and hostess. Oakley's mistress
was in money matters "a shrike." The daughter
ceased smiling as well. Smoke hovered there,

but no flame my nature could discern. One
afternoon he baited hummers by filling flowers
with cordial: besotted, they were easy to collect.
I had taken Dash to fetch wood ducks and later
found the pair on a bench, Eliza staring daggers
at him in silence. Audubon's visage made it plain:
the man was smitten. She was fifteen and asked
why he made so many birds suffer. My approach
hushed them, but the eyes spoke! In September
he slew a rattlesnake, which they drew all day
like demons while the stench increased. He soon
achieved his famous likeness of mockingbirds
defending the nest against a diamondback,
but our sessions were altered, all joy given way
to some distress I denied, fearing my future
might be jeopardized. So runs the world away:
Our brief Eden altered to the realm of shades.

4.
Harvest then, deep evening, all retired, the house
asleep—I rose to answer nature's call. His chaise
was empty. Rushing through rain to the privy,
I was summoned by a nameless force to pause,
then saw a taper at her window, and in its nimbus
his face, the expression fierce as a wolf in rage.
Later, I feigned sleep as he slipped into his sheets,
but there was no dreaming that night, unless sheer
memory of odium amounts to dream. I was certain
I had seen his true nature, but in subsequent days,
when we were dismissed, I pretended to believe:
Eliza fell ill, and with fever season approaching,
Dr. Smith was alarmed, several Pirrie daughters
having perished in years past. To avoid so much
as scandal's whisper, the artistes were allowed

to complete two studies in progress. We stayed
late *au bayou*, surrounded by thousands of wrens,
working beyond dark, dining alone in our room,
by both decree and sentries exiled from the girl,
who in fact had marked faint progress as an artist.
Truth told—this is hard irony—he had amended
her work to "prove" his prowess as a teacher.
So the serpent enters the garden in pleasing guise.
On that matter, also, I held silent, for as witness
to his dark weathers I wished not to invite ire.
Such is ever the law of nature. When we boarded
for the city, Audubon cursed Oakley as "an abode
of unfortunate opulence" and said he had never
been so rudely served. I fathomed why we were
banished and what he'd lost, yet I forged accord.
Could I have been so deep in debt, so entranced
I could not scry apocrypha from gospel? I was
his apostle, and when he whistled, no matter how
perverse the tune, I acted the manikin: I danced.

5.

Our paths crossed years later. I had been retained
to etch native botanicals for Bartram's Garden.
He wore maroon velvet and had trimmed his mane,
no longer hiding his guile behind the Pathfinder's
mask. Gone was the loose suit of yellow nankeen,
the powder horn, and Choctaw knife. No longer
the sylvan heir-apparent of Boone, he swaggered
like an ambassador and carried new girth. Celebrity
can flourish under many a guise. He was courtly,
of course, and offered to send me French wine,
but when I navigated to the unfinished matter
of a share in his success—our wasp nest, yaupon
stalk, my dewy sedge and the sheen from leaves

of mulberry, my excellent muscadines—the famous
man smiled: "Listen, Joseph, most esteemed pupil,
embellishment is necessary but not art's essence.
Your flora decorated a stage while my birds sang.
You provided featherweft, but I am the wing."
Here he gestured to my paintings about the room.
"Now you are ready to stride forth on merit.
An apprentice dwells in darkness until his light
may shine. I gave you shelter, bread, my every
secret." If the school he kept in the woods was
wolfish, the lessons that day were no less fanged.
He called it common practice: "You must not
seek to rise too swiftly, else some hunter's eye
might fix on you." Should I shield his secrets
and live outside history, a shadow accomplice?
I have some pride, and if I am not to share
the profit or glory, let his acclaim, however
ensured, be tainted by a truth. He posed people
as specimens, stifled, with wires. Hawk-eyed
stalker and custodian of beauty, the curator
of God's sweetest gifts, he was less a heron
than a crowned cowbird eager to usurp any nest.
Preening and cutting false trail, he was an agent
of ruin. It was his nature. I must bear witness:
he sought power. To my shame I was besotted
with promises. Where once I spent my vigor
to provide the wild world a mirror that all spirits
might soar, now I am but an absence, a ghost,
and to my regret, even this song of rancor
has ravaged me, my own better nature also lost.

3.

At Shadwell

Shards and hearthstones, letters scratched
by a brant quill dipped in mulberry ink—
all the remnant evidence suggests
the Jefferson children learned minuet
and equestrian manners from "servants"
dressed in livery or crinolines—
when to serve Madeira or hang harateen,
to hunt and dress and elocute like gentry
where empire and frontier met. Clay
pipes and bone combs, a rickle of cat ribs,
a buckle, smudged buttons—all somehow ditched,

while near that threshold dwelled some seventy-six
in bondage, a list including Jack and Jammy,
Orrange, Syphax, two Bellows, Fan (twice)
and Adam, the young master's
personal valet Sawney (also the boy's mentor)
bequeathed to Thomas when his sire
passed. Fenceline, mallet, fleams, and scorched
forks in the dirt attest to an elegance
buoyed on obedience—Minerva, Goliah,
Old Sarah and Quash—each with his mission
in field or house, silence and deference.

Were the Jeffersons so beneficent
from sympathy or just a comprehension
that health and grace of their chattel
bore witness to their status on now-forsaken
acres where once the spit, the rack and cam

allowed a roasted lamb to turn and turn,
its savory flavors ample testament to finesse
and civilization's precise measure?

One cold dusk a nuthatch is tapping while
girls rub the rat-tailed silver with mid-rib
handles, tea steeps in a Jackfield pot,
and the family dines at table, scraping
black walnut chairs across the oiled floor.
The conversation is erudite, spiced with wit.
A scribe should register every nuance, the very
pitch of voices swarming in charmed order,
even as a dropped willow ware saucer shatters.

On a ridge between Three-notched Road
and the swift Rivanna River, in starlight,
all seems grace and elation, as if every soul
here must prosper, all lighthearted as Spring's
myriad purple finches, but those who will never
whisper it have heard of Bates, the new
overseer who on the Snowdon property
whipped poor Hannah to death. Fear simmers,
so no surprise in the quarters that soon a spark

will stray and catch, French drapes blossom
like April flowers, and towers of smoke
billow over the canopy of oaks and poplars,
sweetgums, the whole estate, with one marvel
etched indelible—a gasping Sawney, who rushed
into blazing terror, risking life and limb to save
young Master Tom's red fiddle from the flames.
From his swallowtail coat, smoke seeps.
Also rescued: a legend of enlightened kindness

and for a moment, the painful lives—
Quash, Cesar, Eady, Myrtilla, Leah, Gil
and Nimrod, the two Jupiters, Val and Nell
and Sally, even Hercullus who bathed his face
in heathen fumes and twisted grouse
feathers in his hair to play the wild native after
quaffing pilfered beer. How many will ever
bother to conjure or imagine their toil,
that poise, cautious eyes, the secret names
withheld as the esteemed and much-coveted
Shadwell blazed and roared in a spectacle
to rival Rome's first demise, as it fell?

Priscilla Knight Grinder: Final Affidavit on the Death of the Famous Explorer

"Priss" only to my Robert, your honor, and only
under the quilt when the wick is pinched

dark, but I am not formal by design and will
deliver what morsels I can recall. I must admit

to being well pleased when the Governor bade me
address him as "Meriwether," though the gesture

and name rang equally strange. "Miss Priscilla"
he christened me, but I have been in the roadside

trade long enough to sniff secrets in the air,
and he was a creature surely in thrall to the unknown.

That night I sensed mischief and the tincture of fear.
First, though, this: I saw no evidence of the purse

he was rumored to bear, nor any other bounty.
Listen, sir, he spake to phantoms as an advocate

before the bar or would whisper in corners. He was
surely moonstruck ere he stepped o'er my threshold,

and why not? Three days of deluge, lost pack horses,
a journey we later learned was an affliction.

Our Natchez Trace, oft called Devil's Backbone,
is treacherous, even in mild autumn when Orion

strides visible on his dark road above the bare
oaks, the woods below all copperhead colors,

wild beasts and men fierce with forage.
Much ill transpires in such times, and I was wary

that rumors of prosperity and his elegant uniform
might summon rogues from the road. Yes, yes, in early

depositions I was, admittedly, confused by claims
from men who had been nowhere in proximity.

Conjecture under duress is unlikely to yield
a still water, but he imagined assassins

in every shadow and cowered when not ranting.
Flushed and flustered by officers, I readily admit

to contradiction and revision. I did not witness
murder, suicide or accident, only heard weapons

discharged, as is often the case, regrettably,
at Grinder's Stand. Best, we'd learned by hard

practice, to wait till morning light and sort it out,
else we might throw our own party into jeopardy.

And still, his death is a mystery, buried embers.
I will say this: I hurried into my best calico dress

and exhibited naught but courtesy, the finer
china and cider, though he fumed and rambled

from the go-shot, a man under stress and in dread
for his life. “Liars,” he snarled, pacing the room.

They connived to ruin him or work his demise.
He brandished a brace of pistols. Just ask my

wench Malinda about his comport and disposition,
even as he ate our game stew and the fritters,

honey-laced and fried in bear grease especially
to honor his visit. He was a human storm.

His own servants scattered to the barns for shelter,
but I kept whispering to myself, “hospitality,

Priss,” as I served the high wine and smiled.
Manners? He spilled the salt, cursed and glared

hawk-faced at my children. I ascribed it to long exile
amid wilderness savages, of which we had heard

then only sparse news and rumors, buffalo fables
and tales of silver bears. What was I, humble

matron, to do but humor him and shepherd
my chicks to safety. He asked for my modest

chamber and covered its floor with his bison robe.
Is this what you labor to discover? I brought him tea,

feigned understanding of his gibberish, and when
he finished, retreated to read the leaves in private.

The pattern did not bode well. He was in misery
and sucked his pipe like a man starving, the room

marbled with blue smoke. Rumor claims laudanum,
also, and I can bear witness: he quaffed

some quantity of spirits. True, horsemen passed
in the night. Neelly, a Mr. Russell—I had heard

gossip of various possible assassins. After moonrise
I woke to one of our earth tremors, the children

cowering, the dog all ashiver. Hearsay has it
he carried pox got from the Shoshone squaw

and had sought the previous week to effect self-
murder, but what dawn showed me was the man

lifeless by the door, a pistol in either hand
and two wounds—chest and skull, all now clear

to me. Reek of gunpowder, blood on the puncheon.
Conclusions are elusive, but a man with a broken

soul who had previously failed to work his will
might well aim for heart and head at once.

I can conjecture that the pilgrim I met the night
before might have bid welcome the very hangman,

so whether desperate melancholy or some felon,
the end may have fulfilled his wish. This I regret

deeply, yet know not how I might have assisted. Does
this account illumine the situation? I can promise

with my palm on the Good Book that he commits
perjury and malice who claims Captain Lewis

whispered "Priss" on the verge of his demise,
unless he was wholly demented or aimed

to sully my modest life. What more have I
to offer, your honor? I stand innocent of any

mischief, and if it please you to find our business
finished—though some mystery yet abides,

perhaps beyond answer—my sister and her son
Jackson await, to convey me back to Swan

Farm, a safer place from inquiry and prying.
The servants are today robbing the bees and require

overseeing, my husband due back at last
this very night, so as you surmise, I am eager

to sign my honest name and see the seal
affixed in wax, nothing to add touching on

that disquieting night when I felt the hills
tremble under the bright steps of Orion

and met a man recently returned from the moon.

Fiddler

for Jon Clinch

Most nights this rough customer
lurks by the wharf or in his fishy skiff,
cuddling a jug or hunting one,

but tonight in the auction barn's loft
he stands lightning-rod lean
to wingsaw the rosined catgut

while a dozen giddy couples gallop
and reel to "Troubled by Witches"
or "Sippi Rose." Up close, he reeks

of whisky sweat, piss and snuff,
but dancers in their circles
mark only the sigh and whisper

of his strings. Even old enemies
stamp and swivel to his wicked
licks, but they know he'd steal

the coins from a corpse's eyes.
And the long knife in his boot?
They know the rumors of its use,

though the frenzy he now conjures
is all village bliss and charm.
By dawn the exhausted revelers

will wish him back down river
or in a cell, despite pity for his
woods colt in a patched hat

dozing under an empty bench.
Through "Arkansas Traveler"
and "Death Angel's"

Finn's face like winter driftwood
clenches to cry over the wild buck
and wing: "Stir your ass, Huck.

It's time to earn your vittles.
Bring your old pa the whiskey jug.
Hie up here, ye bastard, and sing."

Pigeons, Pears, Hush

Inevitable and unlikely, yet the Fall River
story excites us still:
                                        a Yankee spinster,
doting daughter (*Once upon a time . . .*), undertaker's
youngest, Sunday school teacher
fond of stoic Job and Joseph reading dreams.

She was not lovely
but raised Shirley poppies the color
of pigeons' eyes.   The summer
insects witnessed: *katydid, katydid, katydid*
        in the trees shading the murder scene.

            Demure in court, she fidgeted with shirring
along her dress front, as ceiling fans and neighbors
whispered.   One afternoon in New Bedford

            before shadowy photos and the prosecution's
rhapsody of disaster, she swore
                        on a Bible once owned by a Mather

that she wore an indigo bengaline gown
        that morning, corded cloth too heavy
for August,
                    submitted in evidence, immaculate,

though Alice Russell next door testified
in full court: the accused burned a blue cotton frock
in the kitchen double
                oven three days after the disaster.

Lizzie was ever fond of blue—
Prussian, cadmium, azure—
and her accounts before the inquest
altered with each repetition
till she settled: I was in the barn
eating sweet pears and heard nothing.
Bridget was performing her chores.
A peddler came to the door, then vanished.

Yet the blood was everywhere, furniture
and curtains, the ceiling! Her adoring father
and depressed stepmother covered, their bodies
axed like Agamemnon and his prophet mistress,
his on the parlor sofa
as if in repose, skull smashed,
left eyeball sliced neatly in half.

No other was home and in motion
but the Irish Bridget scrubbing at the basin,
wiping windows, still ailing from food poisoning,
and not one linen or word out of place,
a house that tidy.

Outsider, intruder, housebreakings of late?
For what other motive? Nothing was missing.

Gentility, the defense asserted, would prevent
a woman, even had she the impulse: love
would always stand in the way.

We know the evidence, no sign of struggles,
the fresh-cleaned axe head (haft missing,
as wood could not readily give up blood traces,
the police skeptical of fingerprint science

and fumbling at every turn).
A history of women in dispute over money,

voices along the staircase, murmurs behind doors.
The ditty convicts her—forty whacks, forty one—
urchins skipping braided sisal as it slaps the dust,
the flawed count less history than myth.

This must be said: the only blood
discovered on her effects was menstrual,
and Lizzie was rumored to suffer spells
when the curse was upon her.

The jury uncertain: evidence inconclusive,
lack of a witness, the woman's demeanor:
she was mousy, the murders grisly.
Women, her attorney implored, possess
divine refinements. She did not testify
(on her counsel's advice).

Was Mr. Borden Scrooge-frugal and cynical,
Caliban in his earthy element,
or just an austere and reticent man,
prosperous in a textile town of humming bobbin
and spindle and dye, where weft
and warp ever intertwine as the shuttle flies,
and who can unweave that mystery,
and what figure looms behind a fine tapestry?

Was Lizzie
(later "Lizbeth," prissy), who relished the theater
and died wealthy,
prone to petit mal when the menses
were upon her? Abuse of a sexual nature,

incest smothered in a hush?
            The fairy tale's wintry stepmother?
Was the bright daughter ineligible
                                                            to be mad or evil?

A temperance household, stiff
with pretension, the deal dressers chipped,
glass baubles from the lamp rims missing.
What's left
                        is a riddle
and acquittal, the mystery intoxicating
        and reenacted to this day. And always

there is the body of Abby, nineteen or twenty
blows, the red and broken form
                        found by the Galway girl despite the veil
of the counterpane's lace.

            Sphinx, Lizzie never broke her covenant
of silence, except to say, stoic in deposition:

                "I was in the barn eating pears,
half a dozen Seckles packed in ribbons
of newsprint, delicious
                                        and not one
drilled by a wasp or touched by Abby
who was never a mother to me."

In the loft her father
                                        had hacked the heads
from her pet pigeons—Saxon pouters and croppers
who swelled to utter
                crew   blue   who — for no reason
ever uncovered. Jealousy?   Her angels.

Feathers soft in the straw.
The axe wedged deep in the salted chopping block.

Later in life she prospered
on the inheritance and took ease in her rocker
on a prestige street
greeting both guests and gawkers,
her parlor clean as a cat's maw,
a brace of songbirds in a cage spacious enough
that they would fly and sing till dusk,

and when she passed at sixty-six

the mourners (curious tourists or friendly or just
church members) remarked:
it never turned one strand gray,
her billow of sternly combed hair which she had always boasted
was strong enough to pull a wagon
and red as a fox.

Special Collections: Girl with Canebrake Rattler

O. N. Pruitt studio portrait, circa 1924

Well-fed, ten or eleven, the cherub
grips her necklace of threat, but her smile
is straight from heaven. She has flung
the reptile over her shoulders like a stole,
and any viewer's invited to lean forward
and guess if the serpent knows his mind.
Together, they seem to carry a message
meant for the desperate and half-blind.
Try as I might, I cannot turn the page.

Pruitt's log reports: "Juvenile portrait,
North Georgia," but the girl in her daisy
dress and curls is no woods colt shackled
in a pantry and brought forth on Sunday
to speak tongues and shake a tambourine.
She shines with the fervor of an elder,
her eyes aware all faith is a darkness
born of stillness and frail light. She is
almost going to reveal the last answer,
and I bend close to hear any whisper.
I don't want to miss a single phrase.

Could Otis Pruitt with his Roitan cigar
and sweaty Stetson smell the grapevine
fragrance or hear the rattles shiver?
Through the glass of the camera's lens
did he find his world suddenly lucid,
even the peril a fit subject for praise?
When the flash bulb's lightning struck,

did anyone flinch or beg for grace?
There she stood, enthralled as a prophet.
Did the canebrake have a truth to offer,
or forbidden fruit or a resting place?

Alive now, this Towne County charmer
would be a hundred, with stories to fill
ten albums, her descendants long settled
and gone Methodist, but her eyes would
still shoot divine sparks that say, "Listen
hard, sugar, the world is deadly, unless
you learn surrender." In that moment
when a shutter snaps to break the spell,
I, too, am fully smitten, for the serpent
is splendid, silvery, the perfect vehicle
for newborn zeal. I almost want to say
"holy," to touch the hourglass of his scales
where time is twisted and suspended.
He does not dart his tongue's dark flare
but holds his pose to see if I am snared.

The girl herself is swimming in bliss,
artless, and I want to breathe it all in:
a studio not far from my native place,
cigar reek, snake-scent of muscadine,
weather of a wildness about to ignite,
the blue blister in the flash bulb glass
and something else, implicit, unseen,
sure to banish any splinter of doubt.

If only the blurred world would startle
awake, I might hear her heart's tranquil
beat and reach out, saying, "Dear sister,
hand me that creature. I am bidden,"

serene while seized by a fiery speech.
But no voice stirs nor rattles shake.
The fading portrait keeps its secret:
snake waiting, the smile. Truth seeker
or tom-fool dilettante, I still ache
for the burning word but fear the strike.

Perfect Pitch

Lexington, VA

A hill child who never swooned Pentecostal
nor marked time to the Sacred Harp,
Ginny Hensley had a voice to send shivers
of regret down any man's spine,
to make every woman tremble in sympathy,
and she heard every note on the Philco
or leaning on her window sill
by Woods Creek, where she learned to pine
for the tremolo of Miss Dixie Dawn
or Anita O'Day's singed sorrow
as Goodman and Dorsey brought velvet
brass and sweet reeds to Lexington
for the fancy college kids to jitterbug
and foxtrot and smooch to.

Years later, when she'd been reborn—
after tirades and tantrums—as Patsy Cline,
she perfected rhythm and tempo,
the dolorous refrain, but drank hard
and talked rougher. "No dough, no show,
hoss," she'd laugh and blow smoke
from her Kool cigarette like a dragon.
"So sweet," girlfriends would witness,
"she'd give you the blouse off her back,"
though they knew not to cross her,
and she delivered those torch songs,
those hurt songs and heart songs
in tones that said, "Be careful.
This honey is scorched."

Forget champagne, Cadillacs and spike heels,
the silver fox stole. She'd slur her words
after hours and remember winter nights
perched like a starved bird at the open sash,
not fancying the Opry, unreal lyrics to "Crazy"
or "Sweet Dreams," but a child keeping time
with fiddling crickets in the grass.

When fans asked about the sorcery
of perfect pitch, her lilt and quaver,
she'd say it was gift and discipline together,
"Walking After Midnight" a complete surprise
that seeped from the soul like stepping
free of a fever, yet "practice and habit" she said:
"It wasn't lightning." A scrapper in business,
she survived lodge concerts and dives
where the hand mic's feedback was
a peacock's scream, but she'd croon
"I Fall to Pieces" till hard farmers, miners
and their weary wives cried.

Radio nighthawks broadcast the icy news
that March morning: the single engine
Comanche had fallen through fog.
Not one survived the fire, almost no trace
of the cherished chanteuse, and the mourning
was general along the hills and hollers,
though few were likely to recall the story:
a girl yearning at the foot of the Blue Ridge
in a stitched cotton gown, risking
a switching to hear mystery whisper
from the open doors of a college hop,
a girl watching for shooting stars
till she felt one calling out—not "Ginny,"

but "Patsy"—her name from the future
rushing toward her through the dark.

Duet

Baylis Richie of Viper,
Kentucky, near skeletal
in this picture with his
famous daughter Jean,
picks a Cumberland
dulcimer with a willow
switch, as his girl's hands

do the same, mirror each
note and drone. He wrote,
"With that music you could
make a mountain ring,"
and today along the Blue
Ridge anyone with a fine
ear can hear, keen eye can

see: peaks he summoned,
forests of spruce, red cedar,
oak and rosewood, any
grain you'd need to shape
a dulcimer, but don't even
bother wishing you could play
hourglass or teardrop zither

as sweet as Jean and Baylis,
who plucked and strummed
as one breath on "Pretty Saro,"
with that magic of kinship,
a gift now nearly gone
to clearcut and ground fog,
hawk call and tainted wind,

all the follies of modern man.
though if you peer hard
enough into this grainy
photo and listen with your
heart's full force, you can, I
swear, hear that whisper—sweet
pea, creeper, trillium, creek

moss and homespun melody
locals still call "blood harmony."
Their pegs? Cut from a poplar.
Fretboards: bittersweet cherry.
Their "Wildwood Flower"—voices
elegant with lore and love—still
echoes through this ornery valley,

sweetens honey, sharpens stings,
makes the blessed mountain ring.

Falwell

[Molly Walker Talking]

Don't blame me, I never gave him that name,
but I saw him once in a roadside meadow
west of Lynchburg, and he was on the ground
under an orphan apple tree, his two minions
deft as chimps high in the branches plucking
the new-ripe fruit and dropping the good ones
into his soft hands. A cloudy-dark Sunday, us
out joy-riding, my Enlo eased his heavy foot
off the gas pedal, and we slowed but didn't brake,
not wanting to gawk but just to be sure we saw
who we thought. He wore a suit Enlo called
"cocoa" but I said "apple seed," and you could
hardly mistake him, jowly, a big grin, new sedan
on the shoulder, a Cadillac as blue as the path
to Heaven. Back then I believed he was not
carving any empire nor partial to pricey cars
or shiny suits, just wanted to spread the Word,
dressed up out of respect for his holy message.
"The Word will burn a sinner," he said on TV.
I sent my monthly checks from the egg money
and stared at him, smiling back, but somewhere
it went bad, him busy in unchristian fashion
working out which group to hate in salvation's
name. Lord yes, I got cured of that habit
some years back, but now I hear he's dead,
his heart given out after so much fried chicken
and inspiration. The Lord had slow torture
for him, long wait with a quick drop at the end,
and it's hard not to trust there was a purpose

in the harm he caused, that some came sweet
to the Spirit, no matter how steep the price,
how angry the sermons or fiery the angel.
You know, I saw a star fall the night we got
the news from Katie Couric, and everywhere
you turned it was tributes and lamentation,
headlines claiming the loss of His right hand,
but I keep going back to a big man in a field,
wild weeds up to his knees, his palms reaching
for something coming from above. On tiptoe,
he was shouting fiery advice at his helpers,
his hair windblown, face bright red. Could be
that's how the prophets work, but so strange
it would be apples, the story, I guess, circling
back to bite its tail. Did he reckon that meager
tree was the heart of the garden? When he bit
hard into the apple he chose out as the best,
did he harvest that godly knowledge we're all
yearning for but fear? It's hard to fashion facts
to say he was either a good man or a mean one,
but like my Enlo said, pushing his foot down
on the gas pedal again, hurrying us to Amherst
before the storm, "I got to hope he'll find peace
at the end, poor devil. You'd expect it nothing
but a burden to walk the earth with that name."
Thunder then, lightning's hiss and fearsome rain.

4.

Rockbridge News, 1892: Breakout

We are distressed to report the Lexington jail
less secure than its architect and good citizens
imagined, despite the multiple obstacles of bars
formed from rails donated by the station master
from the C & O and three sets of forged gates.
The vexing evidence is simple, as yesterday
a pair of miscreants—Caleb Stokes and Willy
Deavor by name—convicted of double burglary
and assault, shoved handguns in the face
of a warden not yet identified, and in a trice
they had cuffed him to a cot and used the keys
to open their shackles and every other lock.
The two seized dusters from the rack and fled
into the morning's fresh snow, but the tracks
were so plain to follow, a posse of eight soon
traced them to the Point Dam along the Maury,
where they attempted to cross, but fortunately
(depending upon perspective) Windle Shaner
had flushed the river just above the locks
to facilitate the ice hardening up for harvest
and the skating parties so popular of late.
His desired effect had not yet been achieved,
so the pair (Stokes sixteen, the Deavor boy
a year his junior) found themselves marooned,
feeling the shifts and spying multiple cracks.
The ferry raft was fetched, but sadly
in the ensuing rhubarb one fugitive began
pointing his weapon, threatening to shoot.
When his refusals to discard the gun turned

shrill, Deputy Jackson Russell with a rifle
tried to wing Stokes but was off his mark
and evidently struck vitals. As his comrade
collapsed, Deavor threw up his hands.
An autumn raft was maneuvered by ropes
and poles. Blood had stained the ice,
and the Stokes boy had breathed his last.
To the dismay of all it was then revealed
that the so-called pistols were fashioned
of soap and stove black. A cortege wended
back to town through wind-blown powder,
snow nearly blinding both posse and curious
bystanders. Absence of conversation was
widely noticed, and Constable Mattice, his
deputy said, struggled to contain his tears.

Rockbridge News, 1892: Porcine Strife

Mr. Bolivar of Snakefoot and Gus Willikins
from Kerr's Creek, running mates and Democrats
since boyhood, possessed of horse sense
and good humor, mostly, have now fallen out
over the taste of true pork and moved quickly
from editorial epistles to fisticuffs, Bolivar
saying the ancient razorbacks do not eat equally
sweet to the pen-raised Yorks, all tallow
but the tail, which is a candle, but Gus swears
with fire in his old eyes that those things
which lurch and leap from precipice to peak
eat with abandon to match a she-possum,
and random carrion taints the meat. At Sugar
Creek Baptist Sunday last, Sandy Bolivar
brandished a rusty pistol, and each cussed
hock and ribs, ham and bacon of his rival's
favorite (Ladybelle Biltshire on the one hand,
Dame Petula Razorridge on the other) until
Brother Spurling stepped in and said Christians
should shake hands and lower the rhetoric's
heat, for women were present, as well as chaps,
and the world does not turn on the quality of lard.
Readers, our wishes ride with that admonition,
but you should beware and keep your distance
beyond handgun range, as riven friendships
mend slowly and heart-felt truce comes hard.

Rockbridge News, 1892: A Lamentable End

We are grieved to disclose details of the demise
of Elder Royster L. Leatherwood late of Smokey
Row and Lexington's First Presbyterian Assembly.
As his neighbors and fellow congregants all know,
R. L. was a man both stern and elegant who would not
deign to cross his threshold in less than a Prince Albert
and Dunlop hat, the sterling ferrule of his mastiff
cane catching every available light, his gold Elgin
and Masonic fob in pocket, even as he sallied forth
to marshal his cows or picnic on black raspberries
along the banks of the Maury. No, he always voted
in Synod on every high matter touching women's
powers in church or out. Severe in speech, he read
Tacitus in the Latin, tithed precisely and was said
to be kind to his wife. Discreet, and yet he enjoyed
being heeded and seen. He pressed the melodeon
on occasion that his children might carol and cavort,
but on matters of theology he was a strict scripture
man, believing the Word delivered from heaven,
no room for exceptions. Assisting at communion
he always appeared serene. On Thursday a week,
R. L. ventured forth attired as a man gone courting
to a meadow he owned near Soapy Run to monitor
the energy of his new red bulls. Perhaps he never
registered the thunderheads above but considered
himself protected from any stormy sky by sheer
faith in his Sovereign and his refusal to relax any
standards, as Mr. Calvin would likely have agreed.
However, when the lightning bolt snaked down
it found his cane and ran through him till he was
briefly—according to affidavit—lit like an advent

candle, and an instant before he collapsed in smoky
char—this from witnesses in a passing wagon—
amid the glowing cloverfield still trembling,
he danced as if in jubilance en route to his final
destination. The ensuing downpour, lamentably,
was unable to prevent his quietus. The deceased
is mourned by Marilise, Brad, and wife Maureen.
The funeral will be held tomorrow at high noon,
Reverend Glinn to offer eulogy and benediction.
Fresh flower tributes are welcome, plus donations
to the Presbyterian mission for fallen women,
a cause for which he often stood as champion.

Rockbridge News, 1892: Avian Complaint

On Thursday last Captain Huss of the fire brigade
was summoned to the farm of Missus Cora Page,
who arrived from Roanoke just two years back
and complained that a red-crested woodhammer,
perhaps drawn to the songbird feeders, had attacked
her cedar board-and-batten walls, affecting damage
and nuisance, making ample racket to imply rapture
or madness. "He might's well be," she informed
the officer, also a near neighbor, "a Maxim gun
like the English use to subdue their Africans,"
and though Huss observed the holes drilled high
on the house, he failed to witness any bird larger
than a ruddock cardinal, finches, puling doves
and dozens of flitty chickadees, so he told Page
his training furnished no solution for such pests.
At this juncture the complainant, a self-confessed
resurrectionist zealot and supporter of candidate
Grover Cleveland, began to rant about unbelievers
and aliens, naming for one Miss Lizzie Borden
of New England who hacked her parents asunder
with a kindling axe, also those Dalton Brothers
of late ambushed in Kansas. "Beings," she said
"should always know their own place and behave
till Jesus comes back." She then chased Captain
Huss to his wagon with a hayrake. He has chosen
to press no charges, since it is known the Page
woman suffers from deep miasma and self-scorn
since her husband vanished, and just a week since
a skulk of foxes savaged her chickens. All this
action transpired on Elk Creek, where on Sunday
Huss found the fresh body of a shotgunned bird

he identified as a pileated woodpecker, its beak
worn blunt with seeking forage in substance
sterner than cedar. Now perhaps Page, even
husbandless, will find some relief. The corpse
of the creature has been preserved for display
by Harvey Beaudreux in Dern's barber shop,
where its scarlet crest and avian grace present
a spectacle, though likely unmourned, it being
evidently insane and not native to this place.

Rockbridge News: Snitch on His Death-bed Relates the Amazing

Watterson Chittum was struck dead by a blast
from Purcell Ruff's shotgun on Saturday last,
the former being in the act of guiding officer
Knight along Varner Lane behind the latter's
sundries shop, the object being a lawful attempt
to catch Ruff selling moon juice on the sly
and effect an arrest, but Ruff claimed alarm
at the sound of evident trespassers by his door
and will plead self-defense at the inquest,
which sadly Chittum will not attend on account
of his demise from the buckshot. Darkness
prevailed in that vicinity, and much is uncertain,
but the greater mystery is this: Mister Chittum,
a Lexington citizen for three decades, a deacon
with the Dove Baptists and livery stable
entrepreneur, went into a species of delirium
before he ferried over the River of Forgetting.
Six witnesses, including this reporter, heard him
whisper that he knew death from an earlier
encounter when he was living as a Thespian—
and not the theatric sort—fighting alongside
doomed Spartans at Thermopylae. "I faced,"
he said, "Persian javelins at the Hot Gates
and fell to the Invincibles, as the oracle vowed
I would. A glorious demise, but it was not
sweet." Then he uttered some syllables we all
agreed might or not be Greek. When they
ceased, he heaved and expired. His brother
Rab, in the shadows all along, stepped forth
and drew Watt's eyes shut with his fingertips.

As one, we looked to Rab, but he dismissed
the Persian story, ascribing the entire rant
to a lifetime of ardent spirits and intemperate
reading, but the balance of those present agreed
it was a deathbed testimony and not so easy
for witnesses to dismiss. "Mishap in self-defense"
Judge Ory ruled the shooting and, slamming
his gavel, advised against the many allures
of wild-eyed speculation and Dame Rumor,
though I have written this and done my duty,
ready to shoulder any fairly reckoned penalty.
For correspondents who would bury neither
truth nor possibility, it comes with the territory.

Rockbridge News: Unexplained Behavior

John Harmon of the Harmon-Bridgewater clan
up in Munch Bluffs and along the North River
was always considered the flower of the flock,
quick in school, then a comer at the tannery,
a Staunch Methodist who liked to pull a cork
but knew how to behave. He had a charming
manner and unmalicious wit, raised Morgan
horses and six kids; a model husband, cousin,
companion in a deer stand, and scarce a soul
could be found to worm a curse his way.
But on October eight he raised a pistol
no one guessed he owned and shot his dear wife
in the heart as she was shelling late peas
on the side porch because, as he told the State's
Attorney, since she started going to the Holy
Rollers, she had taken to calling him "shiftless"
and "sorry" because he called the blessed motions
of God's chosen "dancing" and turned redder
than a Rome apple when he heard another man
had, in open church, washed her feet, which
(again, according to lawyer Beckwith) were
her glory and therefore his. "It struck me,"
he said, "as incorrect and wicked, a genuine
sin, even if it's not in the Book." About what
straw broke the donkey's back he has been
secret, promising to unveil all manner of evil
peccadillos and turpitude sanctioned by those
rogues who practice the holy kiss and claim
to be fluent and preach in tongues never
written. Next Thursday John is slated
to come to the dock and have his fortune

foretold in a quick verdict, which has not
been in doubt since the scent of gun smoke
cleared, though few citizens with the time
to spare deny they want to be there and learn
what their neighbor knows, as suspicions
have long simmered, and the Bridgewater-
Harmons are not known to readily perjure
themselves or circulate frivolous lies. (Her
maiden name was Nix. She was called Hester.)

Rockbridge News, 1892: Owls and Others

On Monday our esteemed Board of Supervisors
held Scalp Day, their annual session to audit
all accounts of the meddlesome animals
brought low for bounty and the general welfare
of county residents, the purpose of this practice
being to balance cost and benefit, also to prove
that ample creature encroachment justifies
allotments for such killing. As always, claims
have been laid for wildcats, skunks, foxes
of both colors, and hawks (over two hundred),
but of especial interest is the slaughter of owls.
Trout Settlemeyer averred that all nocturnal
hunters are noxious, while Dr. Sterling Wirt
took the part of some, saying that though all
large *buboe*s—the hoot and horned foremost
among them—were pests, their lesser cousins
barn and scritch count as our allies, primarily
in the matter of mice, and there are laws
across the Commonwealth protecting them.
"It is best," he said, "to recognize colleagues,
whether in the trees or on this duly elected
and installed board of survivors and never
gun them down for doing their fair work."
His speech brought applause and scattered
laughter, but when he added that chilling
whinnies of owls under a full-blown moon
are meant to remind us of death's nearness,
he lost his disciples, and discussion turned
to a curious item on the list: a so-called goose
owl brought down on Smokey Row by Molly
Berry, a local midwife. The whole Board

expressed astonishment, accompanied
by hissing and scorn, discord from both
parties, but at sunset they voted promptly
and adjourned, having approved their own
actions and glad to escape further inquiry,
leaving this correspondent ill at ease
with a puzzle to baffle ace ornithologists
and perhaps of some interest to local geese
as well as humans prone to goose demeanor.
We are determined to pursue this variety
of beast at any cost to satisfy the curiosity
of readers, hereby enlisted in our quest.

5.

Tube Rose

In spats and monocle Mr. Goober danced
across the blue tin of a Planter's peanut can.
Aunt Emma's rocker kept a cradle's cadence
while the radio evangelist ranted,

"Repent your sins or pay the fiery price."
This was rural Georgia, the Fifties, a "swine
farm" with acres of snakes and corn.
Her voice would waver: "Silver pins and golden

needles will not mend this heart of mine."
She'd spit a golden ambeer into the cess
of her silver-rimmed can and never missed
while Ike was in the White House.

Snuff was cheap, "safe," but the top hat and cane
of the jigging peanut man said "undertaker"
to any Spaulding County child. "The Rapture
is close at hand," the media preacher crooned.

"If your snuff's too strong it's wrong,
get Tube Rose, mild Tube Rose," Aunt Em cooed
to mourning birds courting beyond her song.
A dew of filthy honey on her lip eclipsed

the waning moon. Was such a habit a sin?
She spat and laughed and spoke again
like a devotee of fireflies and summer
love with her lonesome voice that never

made any bashful suitor dance or
lured from cover a single country dove.

Directly

"I'll get to it directly," she'd say, meaning
soon, meaning, when I can, meaning not
yet, be patient, the world doesn't turn upon
your every need and whim. Or "the dogs
will be back home directly, I reckon,"
"the preacher will be finished," "your daddy
will see to you," "supper will be laid out"—
all "directly," which never meant the straight
line between two surveyor's points or
an arrow's flight, but rather, by the curve,
the indirect, the arc of life and breath,
and she was right, and when she passed
or was passing, I could not say which,
in a patchwork quilt, the makeshift room,
the sweet hymn notes sung neighborly
across the hall, she whispered, "Learn to tell
what needs doing quick as a bluesnake
and what will take the patient way, full
of care and mulling, be fair now in every
dealing with beasts and people and all
else alive, and surely, deary dear, He will
come for you in His good time, the way
He comes for all of us, you know, directly."

Beholden

I winced whenever she said it, always
refusing, declining, no matter how stark
the garden, how mere the meat in the skillet,
how low the lantern's kerosene. "I'd not be
beholden to nary a man," was her anthem
of self-reliance, but I always heard it
as confession: "We're from deep country,
not ready to handle debt, you can't trick
us into hand-out shame," though charity
was impressed on me with a switch. "Share,"
she'd hiss while the stripped limb sang
against my shanks. "Boy, you got to share
whatever bounty the Lord sees fit to bestow."
Her words were wrung from the Bible, harder
times than I'd ever know, bitter sacrifice,
steep obligations. "Owing outsiders," she told
my father, "it's a sin, and anyhow, you lose
the higher ground." Bewildered, I was sure
she'd rather suffer death than compromise
her mad pride, though I learned better when
fever knocked me flat and wrung me dry,
my bowels scouring and face red as clay.
While she swabbed my brow with the cold
cloth night and day, she thanked every
neighbor who showed up with physic—
ginger, sorghumed coal oil or home brew.
"Bless you," she'd say, taking the nostrums,
the prayers, the hope, even knowing the old
horse swap was implied, buried in the good
deed, but all the while showing a smile. I'm

bound to say, admiring because I survived:
even in my dreams, crossing the threshold,
that flinty woman was something to behold.

Rogue

Fifteen that summer and mystified by my chemistry,
I'd amble over weekends to visit Newton Hooper,
a mongrel marvel who slouched on naugahyde
in what had been a family room, but now was a trove
of flaking baseball trophies, Stars and Bars throws
on the sofas, a Zenith TV and tilting stacks of stockpiled
girlie glossies—*Rogue Magazine, Frolic, Wink.*
That Saturday he was downing Miller High-Life,
dead soldiers all rowed up to watch the Atlanta Crackers

botch a double-header. His wife Vernell long gone, he was
"batching, a free man at last from a woman too churchy,
and hostile to Chesterfield smoke." He tossed me a copy
of *Knight* with a dark-haired cover girl pouting under her
sampan hat. "Orientals," he said, "you can't lick 'em."
As usual, I eased into the black plaid rocker, blushing,
wondering why he favored the blinds all shut, one lamp
dim, TV down to a whisper, enough smoke curling
along the ceiling to smother any normal mortal. "Meat,"

he told me, "makes the world turn, and don't you forget it."
Opening the shiny pages of the new *Swank* to a naughty
nurse, he held her up, then cowgirls, a pink-nippled pirate
sporting little more than a parrot and a patch. "Look:
they shave them smooth as a peach. These wish book
fellows know what makes men tick, what makes us itch,
us bad dogs, rebels, lobos. Hey, sport, you need to practice
on a beer." Uncapping a bottle, he reached it over,
coughing. I didn't even want to know why I was there.

Outside was all a-swelter, even the magnolia petals

sweating. I sipped, figuring here comes another paradise
lecture on the Miller señorita astride the beer label's new
moon in her frilly skirt and a sombrero I thought witchy.
He liked to preach her virtues, the strumpet cunning
of covering the secret treats and smiling a moon curve
like Wonderland Alice's crazy cat. "They've got the bait.
They mean to catch us. We believe we're the ones fishing.
Shit, Buddy, they sap-suck us dry, and we love it till

they quit, and our hot darling's whisked away overnight
like a fairy story, a prude librarian smirking in her place,
saying, 'Mow the yard, you bum, burn them hornets down.'"
I knew this was the stance of back-room poker palaver
and would rather, I believed, listen to him rant and brag
about his season as a farm team's star fastball reliever
who could pitch a sizzling meteor but never got a break.
"A born liar," my father said. "He'd rather climb a tree
to lip a fib than stand on the earth and deliver gospel truth.

Why do you listen? Is it Dr. Pepper he feeds you, or
bottle beer?" But he never felt the power of Newton's
unrighteous swagger. He'd spit a tirade at the umps, then
stomp around the room. He had a hundred jokes where
smug deacon husbands were gulled and made cuckold
by milkmen, cops, meter readers, Jewel Tea drivers.
"Plow hicks" were his favorite victims. He admired
the scamp who deflowered farmer Donavan's daughter,
then fled a scattergun blast through corn stubble yodeling

"Andyeroldladytoo!" But it wasn't all foul mouth, sports
brag and taboo nudies. He'd been union at the textile
mill, kept peace among doffers, shuttle watchers, pirners,
seamers. He'd blackjack anybody who aimed to settle
rhubarbs with a knife, then laugh in the office with shift

monkeys as they flipped the pages of some high-binding
boss's *Scamp, Cavalier, Rake*. "Some wild damn times,
by God," he said, "and not all the chippies just pictures
on paper." He'd pinch the file girls and steal a kiss here

and there from Nellie, "Orphan Annie" or Ann Tallmadge
Giles, cousin to a senator and wife of the dyer super.
"I'd make believe she was a shameless nun, all nylons
up to the sweet." About then he coughed again, said
cotton lint was in the warehouse air like a snow flurry,
killing them breath by breath. Neither did my father know
Newton's scarred Martin in its coffin case was not just
for show, as he'd tune it up in mid-drunk to howl out
a strike anthem or just tomcat the heartbreak blues,

his best act, but that afternoon his mind was on Santa's
helper in a scarlet cap and coat flashing her pubic thatch
for every gawker with last year's yuletide special *Ace*.
"Listen up, Ally Oop," he said, gripping me by a shoulder,
we got to save you from purity before you're spoiled forever."
He knew a silky woman, older now but still all spice and flair,
who'd show me the ropes, and he'd arrange a rendezvous
then turn me loose to have my cherry picked, my roses
plucked. He'd pay her price, and she had talent, hair

black as a wet crow's wing. He had a room, he said,
where he could keep close watch through a peep hole,
just to see everything went right, but why wouldn't it?
She was nastier than any *Adam*'s monthly Eve and real,
an acrobat. I'd get to prove I was a rascal, scoundrel,
a humdinger, daredevil with a manly future. "Picture
her all sprawled and grinning come-hither. That'll fill
your pencil with lead, make you growl and drool. Time
to bid boyhood adios and get lost in famous pleasures

of the flesh, get your bell rung, boy, your talllywhacker
jacked. First ride's the one you never forget." He said
Lynette worked graveyard shift at Dundee and knew
how to make a bunk bed shake like the loom room
rocking when all the shuttles flew in tune. Suddenly
shy and full flustered, I began to feel needles of regret
and started stuttering about sunset, dinner, chores.
I'd get back to him on his scheme soon. Scowling,
he waved me off: "When you change your mind, sport,

remember, it's my treat, old Newt Hooper's feast."
Next weekend I was on my homemade mound. Pine
sap was nearly bleeding with the heat. I'd wind up, spit,
then pitch the tennis balls over and over at the chalked
strike zone on the barbecue pit bricks, whiffing invisible
hitters from the Barons or Smokies. Crank up, fling,
retrieve, repeat, all the while straining not to look east
toward Newton's house looming in mimosa shade,
aiming to forget the hazy TV and taste of bitter beer

as my curves dropped like shot doves. But my burner
still sang faster than a bee. I wanted to cling to tainted
innocence another season as I zipped the ball knee high,
nicking a corner, or across a phantom batter's chest.
I wasn't ready for the darker secrets but kept hearing
the echo of rogue words: "My treat, free man, my treat,"
as I whispered what I struggled not to picture, "sweet
Lynette," till fireflies sparked random across the yard,
and my fastball sizzled like a meteor through the dark.

Bourbon

My father was hooked on one brand, Ancient Age,
always in pints, perhaps to stow snug in the glove box
with the walnut-handled pistol, and likely to prove
he was a moderate man, and he would tell stories
of his partner Early Thatcher, a devotee of excess,
intolerance, and wrath, who'd slip away from dinner
to take a piss but slink back to the room, sneak a sip
from my father's bottle and add water to hide his habit,
but Early was a steady liar who never in his life solved
a single crime, to hear my father tell it, an improvident
soul prone to nocturnal misdemeanors himself, a bald
rascal who ran with underage women and ate chow mein
straight from the white box with chopsticks, an imposter
who didn't know a six-cylinder from a V-eight.
He short-cutted the Miranda recitation, might slap
a suspect in private and believed the cuffs' teeth were
meant to maim. They both liked their evening libation,
however, and would sit before the TV, sound down
to a whisper, and compare notes, plan the next day's
interviews, searches, and shenanigans. It was arson
they were hired to unravel, usually by pig-wits eager
for the insurance, and I've gawked at many pictures
of the pair in charred ruins, their coveralls streaked
with soot, remnants of an oily rag lifted on a stick,
or pointing at scorched remains of some poor fool
who didn't know his craft and selected the wrong
accelerant or was overcome by smoke. They both
smoked Camels, and Early was portly, a smooth man
who liked his sleep and told blue farmer's daughter
stories when he wasn't bragging, while my father
held himself to one jigger of spirits per evening

and stripped to his skivvies to enjoy his routine fifty
push-ups before retiring. Early got fired, of course,
and my father laughed at the rascal trying to justify
his misdeeds, especially in expense account matters,
but years later Dad confessed he missed the sport
of jockeying to see who'd leave the tip or rush
into a firebug's house first, weapon at the ready.
Then he'd return to the kitchen cabinet and pour
a cool amber dash of Ancient Age, preparing
to reminisce until he'd circle back around
to the pitiful fact that it was Early who opened
my eyes to the darker methods of law officers
and who took me to the range with ample rounds
to fire at human silhouettes until I could deliver
a tight group in the kill zone, at which point I'd
swear with all of Early's extravagant cursing art,
praising the rascal who taught me how to exhale,
squeeze the trigger and shoot for the heart.

Sacred Harp

Like a people of the hatchet, they marked
each fa-so-la with a forearm striking down

through the holy air of the whitewashed room,
as if to split kindling or sever the neck

of the last dinner hen. Their shape notes
in the White book were eggs, flags, diamond

of a rattler's pattern, but Aunt Hannah
told us how the hymns in their hands—

rasped with callous—should have been
anvil, fish hook, sharp ploughshare,

and shuttle. Maybe gravestone or tears.
Menaced by weather and fever, milk sick,

and wild swine trampling the corn,
they'd sit prim in their meeting house

and sweat or shiver in thrall to psalms,
"Mt. Zion" and "Sherburne," "Mear"

or "The Parting Hand." "Sunday,"
she said, "we'd armor weary hearts

with prayer, plain tune and anthem,
men and women just an octave apart."

They made ready for the Father's grace
to blend their echoes for the joyful

noise, "And it was sacred *heart*," she'd
insist, "not *harp*, for only one instrument

was ever hewn perfect to banish
the fiend and seize such blessings

as the hard glory of His sweet storm.
Singing kept us safe, our discipline—

the harmony and 'Amen,' the stern hush—
though I also raised bloodshot hollyhocks,

elegant as tasteful maidens, but lush,
and like the diamondbacks, dangerous."

Within Shouting Distance of the Coosa

Once in Alabama when I was young
and given to aimless ambling,
I followed a red road between pines
where even at midday the cicadas
were complaining, and with nothing
on my mind and expecting nothing,
I was about to pause for water
when the road's weedy roughness
opened to a clearing where boards
wounded by years of weather
formed a modest church, the peak
of its steeple gone and door scotched
open. The wind was scattering pollen,
and somewhere off in the needles
a mockingbird thought it was evening
and half-heartedly sang. Do I need
to say I forced the door and found
everything rain-soaked and broken,
the pews only planks whose cinder
blocks had fallen or were, as I've said,
ruined? But I heard a hum or what
I thought could be a hymn rising
from behind the altar and squinted
to see the worker bees dance and circle
where they'd swarmed. Young
as I was, I understood "not one step
closer, do not disturb," so backed
away, because I knew they believed
their honey holy and would not
suffer it to be troubled without
rushing to beset me, and besides I'd

already been touched by the Word
and held under down at the river
till I heard God's gold voice shining,
insects swarming the choir's serenade,
bee sound the very sound He made.

Maricón

i.m. Emile Griffith (1938-2013), Benny "Kid" Peret (1937-1962)

> "And a man who has found prowess in boxing,
> grant him favor and joy…."
>
> – Pindar

1.
"Whoever controls the breathing in the ring
controls the fight," my father says. Smell of sweat,
Vaseline and bleach, sting of ammonia. "The art

of self-defense is crucial." The gym is damp
and the speed bag singing his beliefs. Elsewhere,
a husky boy from the Virgin Islands quietly

designs hats in a Bronx shop, his chest bare
as he hefts storeroom cartons. His boss says,
"Boy's got a boxer's body," and that begins it.

Emile is bewildered, with no desire for the sweet
science of footwork and fist, no assassin's
eye. When a backyard bully named Jeffrey

lures me to his ring of jeering rednecks,
I clear a path with my ball bat, rush home
to mother, because I'm skinny, afraid. Later,

seeing me teary on the mat at a Scout outing
and pawing feebly at Jimmy Kizner, my father
resolves to plunge me into the discipline.

"To win, you control the breathing," he insists.
Morning roadwork, shadow boxing, mitts.
On his bike, the old man swears as I sweat,

"Your target's never where his goddamn head
is, but where it's going next." Willowy, skittish,
without finesse, I never overcome my fear.

Griffith is a better fit—welterweight, bobcat
quick, graceful as ballet. Coach Gil Clancy
taunts him: "Don't you get that matador strut."

Deft and canny through the fifties, his gold tooth
gleaming and bombshell blondes clenching
his biceps at ringside, the shutterbug's flash

catching the velvet dandy in action,
pearls on his cuffs, satin cravat. Dark mouse
on my brow, I bus back across town

from the gym to mother's tears,
tonic and gin, a dead cigarette. "My other
half ought to know better," she spits.

He travels, sleuthing out insurance fraud
and arson while slick-dealing firehouse
poker. She twists her opal ring, exhales

blue breath. I don't want to be prissy,
hope to show I've got moxie, like a pro,
like that March night when ring pundits

all agree: Peret opened inspired.

2.

Whoever controls the breathing....
Jab and tuck, shoot the right high, hook
to the ribs, drive him to the turnbuckle,

the ropes, the canvas. Griffith has to be
schooled in fury: "It's red sport, boy,"
and rumor has it the insiders suspect

he's keeping a secret, the private life
of linen suits, the pink Lincoln crucial
to his macho disguise. Still, no one

will say "pansy." Control the breathing,
control a rival's will and snuff his soul.
"Wind and feet win it. You have to show

an iron intent": in the garage my father
pops me. "Love taps," he says. "You've
got to learn to shrug it off. Forget thinking.

Make me miss, slugger. Everybody
has a plan, but it's gone to smoke soon
as you get hit. Duck now. Control your

breath, counterpunch, get madder. Murder
me, cream puff. Make me suffer." Years
later, his career over, Emile jokes,

"I like girls and men pretty much equal.
You reckon that make me bilingual?"
He'd known Peret since boyhood, but never

heard those venomed syllables: *maricón*.
I hammered into the heavy bag mummied
in duct tape, pounded that son of a bitch.

"Punish the sap. Maul him up. Make
him miss." Still, my father's snarl....
I skip the rope as it hums, side step,

hop and cross-over, wrists whipping,
weaving, sparring my shadow—left, left
right uppercut. At the weigh-in Peret

keeps whispering what Griffith can't
bear to catch. He guesses the word's
out and starts lurching and whirling,

breathless, shamed. Kid has crossed
the line. *Maricón, maricón*, slur worse
than *tu mama*—"You faggot!" Mild Emile

bides his time. It's sixty-two, my bouts all
history, scuffed gloves and lace-up boots
in a footlocker . . . one local trophy—runner-up.

3.
March 24, Saturday night: Gillette's parrot
cawks about razors—"Feel sharp, be sharp."
The male world seethes: Muriel cigars,

Edie Adams' racy ringside purr: "Why
don't you pick one up and smoke it
sometime?" Her sexy sigh and vixen eyes.

The Garden's a riot of hazed bloodlust,

our Philco's volume high. Mother
flips *Life* in the kitchen with her

sisters, filter tips, a gray kitten. Ruby
Goldstein scolds: "No head butts, boys,
no low blows or rabbits. Protect

yourself, break clean." The pair already
glisten, sponged wet for combat,
breathing easy, both believing, mouth

guards pouting their lips, as if to kiss
and make nice. All a question of mettle
and skill. No one present thinks, "Death."

Bell after bell, circling, sizing up, an even
match for the gaudy belt, the world
sport-smitten, trance-tense, breathless.

A clinic: dole-it-out and roll-with-punches,
clenches, weave, dance, until Emile
finds his moment: no one later can say

how the energy shifts. Rationed breath,
second wind, willpower, a dark gift.
Revived, Emile goes ballistic in the twelfth.

Benny is rubber-kneed, reeling, Emile a man
on fire, windmilling such fury the analysts
go quiet. Some will later say it was only

chance; a few, that a word kept him angry
and whipping in frenzy, making history—
sixteen blows in eight seconds. Others

count it different, but Benny the Kid was
Cuban: "Them Castro boys would possum,"
is the common wisdom, while Griffith's

one rumored weakness is "can't finish."

4.
Sugar Ray claimed Emile was frantic to lay
the rumor in its grave, sew every smirk
shut. I never skipped or bobbed fast enough,

but could hit quick for a white boy—gut
punch, cross, straight shot to the kisser,
a southpaw. I got whipped over and over.

Why did nobody throw in the towel?
Crowd-crazed, Griffith was a tornado,
a blur, oblivious. "I just kept hitting,"

he'd tell a ringside guru still sporting
his blood-spattered tux. "Kid, he didn't
gone down. I kept hitting." Even after,

the specialists said, "a fighter, a soldier,
he'll recover." My father hit the OFF
knob, declaring, "That boy won't fight

again. Neither of them. Animals." For ten
days, Emile paced and prayed. The hacks
wrote, "Benny is a warrior." The coma

ended in a wake and blame—referee,
Emile, even the corner crew who never
lofted the rolled towel into the melee

to ask for mercy. Was it two full years
afterwards with no prizefights on TV?
For decades I never heard the story

behind that word. Years later, leaving
a dance bar called Hombre, Griffith was
ambushed by a dozen and barely breathing

when the siren arrived. A bystander said
they taunted him with: "*Maricón.*
Rise up, boy, show us how it's done

back there in the nigger islands."

5.
Emile had a silk voice, shy eyes, a smile
to lure songbirds from their perches.
He danced with every step he took.

Kid's weeping mother slapped him
in the hospital lobby, spat the word
in his eyes—*maricón*. In his sleep

he saw Benny *perdito*, bleeding from
every mirror and never unleashed again
that stormy combination. History

has nearly erased his name like cheroot
smoke and Edie, Gene Fulmer, Dick Tiger,
Hurricane and Archer. It surely lurks for

everyone, a burning word, forbidden, worse
than split eyelids, bruised kidneys. Is it
yearning for mercy that drives us to misery?

In a world of desperate skirmish and work,
the tear-drop bag still hangs in my attic,
and I will not whip it. Does that win me

a measure of grace? My old man was
nearly right: to beat fear I have to feed anger,
but I pray there's some better purpose for fury

than knocking another man into the dark.

for Mark Sanders, steady ref

Pentecost

for John Foster West

Squint-eyed and cunning, its tongue split
like a wishbone, the canebrake sulls up,
cursive spine and the diamonds in spiral
like genetic code,

and Joby frets the Stratocaster, its plastic
the color of salted ham. A tambourine's
disks shiver, and Brother Pascal wields the blunt
instrument of the Book's hot gospel. This is

spirit. This is bliss. The words from Heaven
would almost strangle you. The Holy Ghost
is a rough customer alright,
and if someone comes for healing touch,

for translation into a mended soul,
a whole body, let him lie beside the altar
all shorn and willing, sing "amen," say
"grace abounding,"

and the current will sizzle, the tail beads buzz,
as the road to Zion is not all gleam-gold.
Wind scratching poplar limbs says
"stormy heart." You can translate any syllable

into yearning, the Lord's will,
as the rattler agitates, this being winter,
his deep sleep stolen by a prophet's
hands clapping. He's a mean

messenger, unguessable, and Brother Harvey
Robbins now cradling him
has the look of a man thirsty for crisis.
Come rapture, come venom,

that double-fang sting so quick you're
not sure at first, then certain. It leaves limbs
chastened, withered. For some of us
in the lantern light, in the Carver's Cove

church house where the floor rattles
like a loom parlor, a coal scuttle:
we know something is coming:
Snake-shakers, Holy Rollers, Faith

Healers from over in Silva or up in Teague.
It ain't no cakewalk to dance against
the devil. Uproot and undercut,
and something is coming right

now, something good. Leave your
coppers and dollars in the collection plate.
The moon out there is empty
as a skillet in night sky.

The snake hisses a new dialect, Hosanna!
On a good night a serpent will crown
some beloved brow like brocade as we
behold jaws open for a kiss. Sister,

keep your eye on the cross, now take my hand.

Ruddock

First time we traipsed beyond Black Lake
Nance said the cardinal she called "ruddock"
was bashful, an ember amid the cedars,
a messenger quick as a hornet, so smart
not even the hungry hawk's eye could track
his madcap path. "Don't trust his *cheer*
and *purty*," she warned me. "To some
he's named bloodbird and brings omens
of suffering to come." I uttered the cluck
of his syllables: "ruddock." It was tart
as an Indian turnip's root. The stark
woods were just thawing, hardwood trunks
dark against evergreens, and we saw one
rushing through the sparse thicket's ice,
his mask mysterious, a seed in his beak,
eyes invisible and scarlet crest sharp.

"You mark me, them feathers has been
dipped in some poor fellow's bleeding.
It posulutely chills my heart to spy one,
but ain't he a beauty?" The evening star
trembled over the bare trees. Next spring
Nance herself was broken and unstrung,
the cough sapping all her piss and vinegar.
Before summer was over she was gone.

Now, when one darts past, I think of Nance
winking, waving her sourwood stick,
winging randomly from notion to notion,
drawling the world to homespun sense.
I picture her ruddy face grinning and speak

the name for that thrum on the tongue:
"ruddock," firebird, that startle and spark.
Sinister or not, it yearns to be sung.

Keelbone

The flag irises were thriving wild in the ditch
near where I was digging their Dutch cousins

and untangling roots to separate clustering bulbs,
when I uncovered in the loose dirt a twist

of bones and fluff, most bits broken—wishbone
called *furcula* in field guides, also the *ischium*,

some ribs and skull chips. Buffed between my fingers
they were a small shipwreck, the most prominent

artifact a keeled sternum, its carina sharp,
the whole bone saying *vessel* and *steady*.

I knew it as the anchor point for the wing
muscles of what, from size and the usual

traffic, I took for a small crow or songbird fallen
the year before, its skeleton riven by appetites

and more sinister forces. Yet here was one
bone, a keel, a ploughshare for parting wind

or water, apt prow for any hazardous journey,
and how it shone, a blinding blue-white to put

any wildflower to shame. Rubbed on my cuff,
spit-shined, it was a relic of every dream

of flying I ever harbored. Can I say I felt my
own sternum sharpening? Would it seem

too much like lying? Clavicles and flight bones—
was I about to rise? The flag irises were

bowing with weather, sky overcast then,
re-setting the bulbs in earth not half so urgent.

Considering a new direction, I pondered
the wayward keel in my palm and listened

for crow calls in the near yonder saying,
"Come hither." My allegiance has long been

to the flowers, but as a boy I slept on feathers.
Now, I thought, is the right moment to rise—

in the spell of keel, plough, cloud—and sing
whatever song I had always been missing.

I felt a lifting. I swear this is not lying.
It is not nonsense. I might yet soar.

Owling

All month I'd been hearing them call
from the woods of a neighbor, an angry
fox-faced man who in my judgment

deserved no owls. They were a blessing
in the record heat, their whinnying
voices like young horses in the distance,

and I'd sit at twilight by my high window
and wish they'd approach, until at last
one dusk a soundless wing passed beyond

the trees. At first I knew it was a bird
but never guessed which species, since
screech owls are secretive, built for stealth

and lethal surprise. The open window
allowed me to hear the slightest wind
in the lean hickory—eight, maybe ten feet

from my face—and when the first owl
lit there, I froze, perhaps as a rabbit
will pause if the shadow falls across her.

The limb scarcely stirred with the weight,
and it stared straight at me, swiveled
its head, preened, then seemed to dance,

first one foot, then the other rising, eyes
locked to mine—curious, quiet, unafraid.
It was amber-eyed and in gray phase.

I knew under those powdery feathers
the body was smaller than a dove's
and was thinking how I might cup it

inside my hands, but I'd also heard
they're fierce, willing to protect a nest
by striking something large as a man.

Soon the bird uttered a lonesome call
toward the nearby locust, but remained,
gazing at me with tufted ears twitching,

until I heard my neighbor screeching
for his children to come home *Right now*!
his voice shrill not with anger but worry

and yearning, and I thought, despite
his tantrums and gall, he needed owls,
as the issue, after all, has nothing

to do with deserving, perhaps even
less with wanting, because on the sill
of darkness we will all stand equal,

in need of the world's heartening trill.

Shades

When Odysseus descended to the underworld
and crossed the dark river to learn the key
to his destiny, he poured the ritual milk and honey,
the wine and barley and blood to summon the dead,
but he never expected to find his mother among
the shadows who were filled with mist and sifted
with the wind which had no source. He had thought
her alive and back in Ithaca expecting his return.
He had assumed the worst ordeals were his own.
But when he reached out, shivering as he wept,
to embrace the ghost, that wanderer found
no substance, no flesh nor blood nor bone,
and he must have felt as I did that first time home
when my mother's mind had begun to wander
and she disremembered not only the laughter,
the lightning-struck chinaberry, the sunset
peaches and fireflies and the sharp smell
of catfish frying, but also her name and the fact
that she was sitting in her kitchen of fifty years
beside my father who stood there straining
not to wring his hands or surrender to the tears
welling around his eyes. She gathered her purse
her hat and wrap, then said, "Please drive me home
before strangers take every damned thing I own."
Her eyes glaucous with terror, she was exhausted
and desperate, almost herself "an empty, flitting
shade," as Homer says it, uncertain in her haze
whether she was moving toward or away
from what might be called the Great Dream.
When she sobbed and cried, "Where is my son?"
I, too, felt bewildered, and not even a seer

from the land of night and frost and smoke
could tell me what words would amount
to comfort nor which constellation to steer by,
nor where all this heart sorrow might end.

ACKNOWLEDGMENTS

Appalachian Heritage ("Beholden")
Appalachian Journal ("Perfect Pitch")
Arts and Letters ("Owling")
Asheville Poetry Review ("Rogue")
Atlanta Review ("Impasto")
Cincinnati Review ("Major Henry Rathbone")
Five Points ("Tube Rose")
Georgia Review ("Girl with Canebrake Rattler")
Louisville Review ("Falwell")
Missouri Review ("Gloves," "Summoning Shades," "A Serpent's Tooth")
Notre Dame Review ("Pentecost")
Oxford American ("Directly")
Pleiades ("Within Shouting Distance of the Coosa")
Poet Lore ("Keelbone")
Prairie Schooner ("Maricón")
Sewanee Review ("Mendicant No More," "Ruddock," "Shades")
Southeastern Review (Selections from "Rockbridge News, 1892:" "Porcine Strife," "A Lamentable End," "Avian Complaint")
Southern Humanities Review ("At Shadwell," "Lizzie Keckley," "Pigeons, Pears, Hush")
Southern Poetry Review ("Flower Coffin," "Bourbon," "Priscilla Knight Grinder: Final Affadavit on the Death of the Famous Explorer")
Southern Quarterly ("Mockingbird," "Sacred Harp")
Southern Review ("Fiddler," "Still Life: from the Notebooks of A. Bierce, 1862"; "Henry Kyd Douglas, After Cold Harbor")
Waccamaw "Owls and Others") *Rockbridge News*, 1982

The following poems were reprinted in *Poetry Daily* (poems.com): "Shades," "Bourbon," "Within Shouting Distance of the Coosa," "Keel Bone," and "Duet."

"Bourbon" was reprinted in Volume 19, Number 1 of *Southern Cultures*, 2012.

"Pentecost" was reprinted in *Best American Poetry 2008*, edited by Charles Wright.

"Mariçon" was reprinted in *Best American Poetry 2017*, edited by Natasha Trethewey.

The three poems in the "Mary Lincoln Suite" received the Perkoff Prize from *Missouri Review* and were reprinted in *Lincoln's Lover: Mary Lincoln in Poetry* (edited by Jason Emerson, 2018).
"Keelbone" was reprinted in *"more truly and more strange": 100 Contemporary American Self Portrait Poems* (edited by Lisa Russ Spaar, 2019).
"Pigeons, Pears, Hush" received the Theodore Hoepfner Poetry Prize from *Southern Humanities Review* in 2011.

The author would also like to thank Don Selby and Diane Boller, Philip Belcher, Davis Enloe, Natasha Trethewey, Charles Wright, Speer Morgan, Steve Corey, Mark Sanders, David Bottoms, E. Ethelbert Miller, Jody Boltz, Kirk Follo, Don Secreast, Brendan Galvin, James Smith, Marc Jolley, and Sarah (always).